Stealing Glances

stealing
Three Interviews with Wallace Stegner
glances

James R. Hepworth

University of New Mexico Press
Albuquerque

Library of Congress Cataloging-in-Publication Data

Stegner, Wallace Earle, 1909–

Stealing glances: three interviews with Wallace Stegner/
James R. Hepworth—first edition

    p. cm.

Includes bibliographical references.

ISBN 0-8263-1835-5 (cloth)—ISBN 0-8263-1988-2 (paper)

  1. Stegner, Wallace Earle, 1909– —Interviews

  2. Authors, American—20th century—Interviews

  3. Historians—United States—Interviews

  I. Hepworth, James R., 1948–

  II. Title.

PS3537.T316Z469   1998

813'.52—dc21

[B] 98-22302

CIP

Designed by Sue Niewiarowski

CONTENTS

ACKNOWLEDGMENTS

Although this is only a little book, it needed a lot of
help to become a book at all, and I want to thank those
who made its making possible.

First, aside from the unpayable debts that are most
obvious, these interviews owe their existence to Tanya
Gonzales, who provided me with the opportunity to
conduct them. She also encouraged me to think of these
pieces *as* a book and to send them to Beth Hadas at UNM,
who became their steward. May the last now become first.

A grant from the University of Arizona's Graduate
Student Development Fund paid for my first trip to Los
Altos Hills to interview Wallace Stegner in his natural
habitat. An advance from *The Paris Review*, where a portion
of these interviews first appeared, permitted me to make
a second trip. For frequent transportation from airports,
museums, bookstores, and bars in the Bay Area to the
home of Wallace and Mary Stegner, I'm indebted to Marc
and Wendy Brown. My thanks also to Tom and Marilyn
Auer, publishers of *The Bloomsbury Review*, for publishing
brief excerpts and to Ed Dryden and Richard Etulain for
their thoughtful and considerate reviews of the manuscript.

Jeanna Brown patiently helped me prepare the text, and
Sarah Green's library research on my behalf permitted me
to check a few facts. During the time it took me to write
the introduction, Myrlin Hepworth had to become the

captain of our ship, and I thank him for swabbing decks and manning the galley while I wrote and revised.

And finally, thanks to Dick and Lois Shelton for loaning me Wallace Stegner's books and introducing me to Wallace and Mary Stegner in the first place.

STEALING GLANCES

When I recorded the first of these interviews on 14 April 1977, in the Terrace Lounge of the Student Union Building on the campus of the University of Arizona, I was still in my twenties. Wallace Stegner was sixty-eight. By young people's standards he was already an old man, and he had a head of thick, silver hair to prove it. Still, so far as I could tell—and I did my callow best to judge him immediately—Wallace Stegner did not talk like an old man. Or walk like an old man. Or even look like an old man. And he was taller than I had imagined him, well over six feet. Despite his hair and his conservative dress—light suit coat, off-white shirt, plain dark tie, dark slacks, wing tip shoes—there was very little old about him. On the contrary his physical presence radiated energy and strength. Of course in conversation his disinterested goodwill soon proved to be the product of extreme erudition and the wide personal experience of his maturity. Just looking at him, though, it was obvious at a glance that while aspirants like me lived mostly down below ground, where we tried to avoid the hissing and barking and snapping of jaws that constantly went on just above us, Wallace Stegner lived his life like a bird, well up in the sunshine. Both his hands and his face were deeply tanned. He smiled often, and when he smiled his milk-pale blue eyes sometimes glittered with mischief. His voice, which exuded confidence, was richly endowed: smooth, pleasant, and mellow, like a musical instrument—or a good bourbon.

"Hello," he said when Lois Shelton, the director of the

Poetry Center, introduced me. Lois explained that I would, with his permission, be taping the question and answer session. "Fine," he said and extended his hand and arm toward me. Without thinking, I took the hand in my own.

I wish I could say that something galvanized me in the two seconds it took to shake that hand, that I felt the same kind of electrical shock that I might have felt if I had just touched a live wire and been bitten so hard by the current that I was almost unable to let go. I could almost accept that exaggeration because it contains grains of truth. Wallace Stegner was a guardian spirit. Through his books he had already passed something of that spirit on to me and everyone else who read him. But that moment we met was also something special. Our meeting, in fact, literally changed my life. What's more, both in his person and in his writing it was his particular genius, as Gretchen Schoff notes, to "take dailiness"—something like a handshake—"and turn it into transcendence" (41). Exaggeration, however, absolutely belies the entire character of a man who always presented himself and his work on a level playing field. Because he believed so profoundly in human dignity, he treated people with consideration. "In a sense," his son, Page, says in his preface to *The Geography of Hope* (1996), "we were all his sons and daughters, uniformly treated by him in equal measures of affection and respect; treated not as acolytes, students, underlings, the less accomplished, but as peers. Because that, indeed, is how he essentially perceived us" (vii).

As I've just tried to make clear, however, that is not the way I perceived him. And judging by the testimony of others of my generation, especially mutual friends and acquaintances such as John Daniel, T. H. Watkins, Charles Wilkinson, and Terry Tempest Williams, that is not the way they perceived him when they met him, either. While none of us ever went so far as to start introducing ourselves to other people by saying, "Shake the hand that shook the hand of Wallace Earle Stegner," I think everyone who knew his work was always just a little intoxicated by his presence, and that first moment was, at least for me, exhilarating. The next thing I knew he had settled himself into one of the room's low-backed swivel chairs, even the boldest of the undergraduates in novelist Robert Houston's beginning fiction class had withdrawn into a nervous and obtrusive silence, and I had already asked my first question.

Looking back on that afternoon now, precisely twenty years later, it is easy for me to see that I exploited my own temerity and the timidity of the undergraduates to question Wallace Stegner, without interruption, for almost an hour. Finally Robert Houston asked a question or two himself before I continued and ended what I'm afraid may have seemed to Stegner more of a cross-examination than an interview. In *Beowulf*, however, we learn that Fate will sometimes spare a doomed man if his courage is good. Besides, if I was being brash and inconsiderate of others by asking too many questions, Wallace Stegner was not. As he spoke he gestured frequently but leisurely with his long, rangy arms and hands, and more than once he made full eye contact with every person in the room. There must have been about twenty of us literally seated at his feet on the plush carpet. Occasionally he also paused at the end of a response and swung himself gently toward one or another of his undergraduate listeners, in anticipation of a question. When none came, he quickly surveyed the room and then turned back toward me. Sometimes he nodded kindly at me, like a gentleman passing another gentleman on the street. At other times a half-smile of apparent bemusement played at the corners of his lips and eyes. Whichever it was—the nod or the smile or the lift of a hand missing part of one finger—I took my cue and asked the next question on the long list I had prepared. For me the day of my first meeting with Wallace Stegner was the beginning of a great adventure. For him I suppose it could not have been much more than another ordinary day in paradise.

Certainly, I was lucky to meet him when I did.

For one thing, back in 1977 he was already six years into his so-called retirement from Stanford as Jackson E. Reynolds Professor of Humanities. In some ways he was at the height of his powers. The day before we met, for instance, the winners of the National Book Awards had been publicly announced. Those of us connected to the Writers Workshop at the University of Arizona had been especially excited to learn that the prize in fiction had gone to our visiting author, Wallace Stegner, for his eleventh novel, *The Spectator Bird*. We all knew that he had already won a 1972 Pulitzer Prize in fiction for *Angle of Repose* (1971). What we did not know was that two years before, in 1975, he had just missed winning a second Pulitzer Prize (this one for his biography of Bernard Devoto, *The Uneasy Chair*) by the narrow margin of a single vote. Without any reaching after guilt or justification, or so it struck me then, Wallace Stegner could easily afford to follow his personal inclinations wherever they might lead. In other words, I believe I remember thinking to myself, he can do whatever the hell he wants to do whenever and wherever and with whomever he wants. He was, I reckoned, just about as safe as a justice on the Supreme Court.

That's how little I knew about freedom, not to mention Wallace Stegner's sense of responsibility.

Thinking back to that time in his career after studying it now for two decades, I keep wondering what his personal and private inclinations really were and how often he did, in fact, get the chance to pursue them without interruption. Even after rereading Jackson Benson's authorized biography, as I've lately done, it is easy to forget how much of himself Stegner gave to the world and difficult to know how much he kept exclusively for and to himself and his family. For instance by the time he got around to "retiring" in 1971, he had been teaching for nearly forty years, first as a graduate student at the University of Iowa, where he received his M.A. in 1932 and his Ph.D. in 1935, and continuing at Augustana College, the University of Utah, the University of Wisconsin, Harvard, and Stanford. At Augustana, he was fired. At Wisconsin, it is still rumored today, Wallace Stegner was passed over for promotion in 1939.

Not true. While Wisconsin refuses to promote Stegner's fictional narrator, Larry Morgan, in *Crossing to Safety*, in point of fact Wallace Stegner left the University of Wisconsin of his own volition. He spent the next six years teaching at Harvard University (1939–45). And from Harvard he came to Stanford, where he founded what turned out to be, arguably, the best creative writing program in the United States and where he continued to teach for the next twenty-six years (1945–71). His "general schedule," he told me in our second interview, "was to teach a full load of courses in two quarters in order to get two quarters off in consecutive order." Even granting Stegner's leaves of absence—he received three Guggenheims (1950, 1953, 1960), for example—forty years is a long time to be teaching. Maybe even "too long," according to Wally. "I didn't retire from Stanford," he privately reiterated during the course of these interviews. "I quit. I'd had a bellyful."

Those words make him sound far more discontented than he actually was. While he wished he had been able to quit teaching sooner, he obviously took a quiet pride in the program he had built almost single-handedly at Stanford, if only because it had helped so many writers (far too many to name here). "You're very fortunate to have the university," Stegner says point blank in our first interview. "Many people don't." In fact, judging by his books, the Stegner ideal is probably a town of modest size with a university in it, preferably (although not necessarily) somewhere in the West. As he observes in his foreword to *The Uncommon Touch* (1989), too many American communities are "intellectually and culturally and artistically inert" because they have no "academy to leaven their lump." He then points to places that "take most of their character from the academies they foster. . . . Princeton, Chapel Hill, Charlottesville, Amherst, Palo Alto, Berkeley, Cambridge, New Haven." Take away their "intellectual cores," Stegner writes, and these small cities would "shrink like Alice at the entrance to the rabbit hole." The suburb or town in which a great university is set "takes on a glow" because the university not only can offer "the best that has been thought and said in the past" but also "the key to the future." Writers in particular, he says, "need both tradition and freedom. They have to know where their society has been before they can handle the language and the relationships out of which they will make their fictions and poetry. And minds grow by contact with one another, the bigger the better, as clouds grow toward thunder by rubbing together" (xvii).

Of course in addition to being a lifelong writer and teacher, by the time I came to know him, Wallace Stegner had also, like his friends Bernard DeVoto and Robert Frost before him, become a public figure and therefore a public force. What he said both in and out of print mattered. As most of his readers know, he came to public service, however reluctantly and most auspiciously, in 1961, after President Kennedy's secretary of the interior, Stewart Udall, persuaded him to become his special assistant. From 1961 through 1966 Stegner served as a member of the citizens advisory board for the national parks and monuments, chairing the board his last year. In addition, from 1964 until 1968 he served on the governing board of the Sierra Club during what his biographer believes may have been the most difficult and fractious time in its history. The conflicts that erupted during his tenure on the council, especially between his friends David Brower and Ansel Adams, made him resolve never to serve in such a capacity again, and yet the Reagan administration's assault on the environment so alarmed and angered him that he joined the Wilderness Society's Governing Council in 1984. He also held long and active memberships in Phi Beta Kappa, the American Academy of Arts and Sciences, and the National Institute and Academy of Arts and Letters.

How, I always wondered, did he ever find time for someone like me, for soon enough I became a minor but frequent inter-

ruption myself. Almost immediately after his campus visit,
I began to write him letters and call him on the telephone.
Within a year I had enlisted his support on a project. Then,
I suppose inevitably given my own selfish character, I began
to call or write just to get his advice on personal matters.
Eventually he became the subject of my dissertation on
Angle of Repose. Before I completed it, with the help of his
recommendation I landed an assistant professorship at a
small college in Idaho, where I also became the publisher
of Confluence Press. At Confluence I was lucky enough to
commission and publish some of his last essays, including one
each on Norman Maclean and Wendell Berry. Best of all and
regardless of when it happened between the time we met on
14 April 1977 and the time he died on 13 April 1993—almost
fifteen years later to the day—Wallace Stegner not only became my mentor, he became my friend. In simple terms he
made me feel good, wanted, loved, even important and happy.

Looking back to that first day, though, I suppose part of
what most amazes me is that in 1977, despite having won
nearly every major literary honor open to an American except
the Nobel, Wallace Stegner at the age of sixty-eight had yet
to fully achieve himself as a writer. He still had, for example,
two of his best novels inside his head: *Recapitulation* (1979) and
Crossing to Safety (1987). In addition to four monographs and
two collections of interviews, he would go on to publish six
more books in all. For most people the work Wallace Stegner
accomplished between the ages of sixty-eight and eighty-four
would constitute an entire career—and a distinguished career
at that, one supplemented not only by the continuing flow of
prizes and awards and critical acclaim, but also by more than
a modest amount of commercial success. All three of his last
books, for instance—*Crossing to Safety, Collected Stories* (1990),
and *Where the Bluebird Sings to the Lemonade Springs* (1992)
—made the bestseller lists.

I think his controlled passion for novel writing in particular
and literature and history in general partly explains his slight

preoccupation in the first of these interviews with the state of publishing in the United States. He didn't like what he was seeing. To his way of thinking, what a 1997 issue of *The Nation* calls "The Crushing Power of Big Publishing" was already generating far too much power and becoming a destructive force. "Publishers get timid, like Hollywood movie makers, trying to reproduce successes only and never taking chances," he says early in our first interview. Consequently, he implies, they produce a lot of duds. Later, in 1982, on the deck of his home in Los Altos Hills between the recording sessions for our second interview, he told me that even his agent, Carl Brandt, had resisted the idea that a novel of the Jazz Age could be set anywhere in the interior West, but especially where Stegner set his—in Mormon Salt Lake City. Brandt resisted the idea, of course, because he was afraid he couldn't sell it. Once it was published, *Recapitulation* went on to sell twenty-three thousand copies in hardcover through four printings in less than two months. Eighteen years later, it is, remarkably, like almost all of Stegner's other books, still in print. I say "remarkably" because these days the life expectancy of a midlist book from a New York publisher, which is about the only kind of book Wallace Stegner ever published, is roughly equivalent to the shelf life of yogurt, as the *New York Times* recently put it (7 July 1997).

Be that as it may, by the time I got around to taking Wallace Stegner up on his invitation to visit him, five years had elapsed. In that five-year interval, he had not only published *Recapitulation* but also a book of history, *American Places* (1981), with his son, Page, and photographer Eliot Porter. He had also written and published a limited edition monograph entitled *20-20 Vision: In Celebration of the Peninsula Hills* (1982), and his second collection of essays, *One Way to Spell Man* (1982), was just about to come off the press. In addition two important books about him were also near their publication dates: Anthony Arthur's gathering, *Critical Essays on Wallace Stegner* (1982), and Richard Etulain's *Conversations with Wallace Stegner on Western History and Literature (1983).* The first full-length work devoted to his life and writing, by Forrest G. and Margaret Robinson, had appeared the year we met as volume 282 in Twayne's United States Authors Series under the title *Wallace Stegner* (1977).

Perhaps needless to say, during the five-year interval between our first and second interviews, the political climate in the United States had drastically altered. President Jimmy Carter, elected in 1976, had just begun serving his first term in 1977 and had been about to ask Congress for new legislation to discourage waste and encourage conservation measures. He was, in fact, waging an all-out campaign for energy conservation, which he called "the moral equivalent of war." By the time Wallace Stegner and I met again in person on 1 March 1982, Ronald Reagan had already appointed James Watt his secretary of the interior, proposed his famous 10 percent income tax cut, called on Congress for an astronomical increase of $5 billion in defense spending to fight the Evil Empire, and our nation was well on its way to the kind of deficit spending that so deepened our national debt that we may yet end up impoverishing our grandchildren.

On the other hand, multiculturalism and Women's Studies were everywhere in the air, and in English departments across the land they were blooming into something almost as fashionable as critical theory. "Should I take an interest in you even if you *were* historical, white, a woman, and my grandmother," Stegner's narrator, Lyman Ward, rhetorically asks himself in *Angle of Repose*. I was beginning to ask the same sort of questions about Wallace Stegner, who was not only historical and white, but also a man.

By now several things in particular had begun to occupy my thinking in regard to Wallace Stegner and the West. I began to realize why I reacted so emotionally and so powerfully to his work: Wallace Stegner wasn't so much telling his readers who he was as how to find out who we were. Like him I had grown up deep in the interior of the western United States, in what he would later call, in *The American West as Living Space* (1987),

"the last of the sticks." Not only that, but I had lived in some
of the very places where, as he put it, "the stickers had stuck":
most notably in predominantly Mormon towns and on Indian
reservations. In 1852 my paternal ancestors had come to Salt
Lake from Liverpool, and although I was an apostate of the
first order, I had learned to respect and even admire the cohe-
siveness of Mormon culture.

On the other hand, when in about 1980 I first read Stegner's
Mormon Country (1942) as a graduate student in the Ph.D. program at Arizona, I thought it frankly nostalgic and naive, as
unworthy of the Wallace Stegner I knew as were some of the
other arcane products from his pen that I had begun to un-
cover. *The Potter's House* (1938), for example, was clearly one
of those aberrational novellas by a writer in his twenties that
are best left to the dustbins of oblivion, not unlike Edward
Abbey's *Jonathan Troy*. Stegner's third novel, *On a Darkling
Plain* (1940), I found heavy-handed and full of awkward and
abrupt shifts in point of view; his fourth, *Fire and Ice* (1941),
impressed me as nothing more than a potboiler. When I asked
him about these books one day on the telephone, to my surprise he listened respectfully and more or less agreed with my
assessments. Then he told me he had no intention of allowing
anyone to reprint them.

I confess, however, that I read *The Gathering of Zion* (1964)
with more than passing interest. For the first time that I knew
about, someone had taken on the Mormon creation myths
and turned them into living history. I think even Mormon
historians must have realized how important it was to have
an outsider tell their epic in classic narrative style and in
dispassionate prose, especially the chapters of their exodus,
the great migration; and because it was *my* past that Wallace
Stegner chronicled, I think for the first time in my life I began
to actually acquire what I had assumed I already owned—a
sense of history and therefore a sense of myself as a particle in
the stream of civilization. And then, of course, I was hooked.
I began to understand the Stegner novels I admired, especially

The Big Rock Candy Mountain (1943) and *Angle of Repose* (1971),
as history and to perceive history, in synthetic DeVoto and
Stegnerlike fashion, as literature.

I also began to understand something that I think more and
more people are eventually going to have to admit. Wallace
Stegner became a new kind of American writer, one who, in
his student Wendell Berry's words, understood "remembering
as a duty" and who therefore understood "historical insight
and honesty as duties," a writer not only with a profound
sense of place, but a writer who did his best to protect that
place "by writing and in other ways, from its would-be
exploiters and destroyers" (16). In many ways he was the very
antithesis of the stereotype and popular image of the writer
in America. He was, for instance, neither suicidal nor manic-
depressive, alchoholic, egomaniacal, nor even a little bit crazy.
His best novels are quiet, internal dramas fashioned from
reality, and women figure into them on about the same foot-
ing as men. To many, Stegner's last novels—*Angle of Repose,
All the Little Live Things, The Spectator Bird, Recapitulation,
Crossing to Safety*—appear conservative, for some of their
strongest themes are fidelity, marriage, and family. I believe
they are, in fact, revolutionary, if only because they restore
a lost balance to American fiction, which turned inward
on itself, into what John Barth called "The Literature of
Exhaustion," all through the 1960s and 1970s.

To the literature of the American West, Stegner's novels
and essay collections add some things that many of us Anglo-
Americans who came of age in the West would never otherwise have received in sufficient measure, at least not in a
literary way: a society that can almost match our scenery and
a true connection between an authentic past and an inherited
and inhabitable present. One of the most important issues that
Stegner discusses in these interviews is probably the lack of
a "usable past." "We are the unfinished product of a long
becoming," he wrote in his foreword to *American Places*. "In
our ignorance and hunger and rapacity, in our dream of a

better material life, we laid waste the continent and diminished ourselves before any substantial number of us began to feel, little and late, an affinity with it, a dependence on it, an obligation toward it as the indispensable source of everything we hope for" (vii).

By contrast, he wrote in the next paragraph, although they were "often guilty of primitive assaults on the land, principally the setting of wildfires to run game or improve the grass, Native Americans did feel a reverence for the earth and its creatures. Their descendants feel it still; the earth is at the heart of their religion" (vii). "The western habit of taking charge of one's environment and doing things to it and fixing it is very much under challenge and attack," he told me in 1977. "That's partly due to environmentalism, it's partly due to notions learned from the American Indians, and its partly due to the quietism of Zen. . . . I'm all for it. . . . Indian attitudes toward the earth seem to me healthier than white attitudes, by and large." Yet one of my favorite Stegner critics, Elliott West, notes in a 1996 essay that "Stegner wrote remarkably little about Indians" (67). The question, in this moment of political correctness, is why.

The answer, I think, is fairly obvious and goes back to Stegner's comments to John Milton in 1969 (published in 1985). While acknowledging the "great intuitional sensitivity" of William Eastlake's *The Bronc People*, Stegner also recognized the genuine disadvantages of "trying to write about Indians from a non–Indian point of view." He comments to Milton, "Scott Momaday's got the edge on all of us there." "The reliance upon an Indian view of nature in which you can depend upon something long and tested—not a kind of tourist's view and not a reader's view but a real inhabitant's view," Stegner pointed out, is "hard to come by in lots of the West" (108). And so it was. As good as novels about Native Americans by non–Indians might be, Wallace Stegner knew enough to believe in the real thing.

In other words, Wallace Stegner took the long view on this

issue as well. As a student of American history, he knew there was some truth in Flannery O'Connor's idea that the South had developed so many good writers because it had lost the Civil War. In 1969 Stegner was already looking ahead to the day when American literature would finally come of age and American Indian writers would not merely exist but thrive and flourish. By 1982, when I flew from Tucson to San Francisco to meet Stegner at his home in Los Altos Hills, Scott Momaday had already officially become one of my teachers, but just across campus was another Indian writer, Vine Deloria, Jr., whose office was always open to me as well. Leslie Silko had just left the English Department after being granted a fellowship along with Robert Penn Warren in the first round of the MacArthur Awards. A young Arizona professor named Larry Evers and I had, along with Dolle Noche, Dan Brudevold, Ofelia Zepeda, and others, resurrected *Sun Tracks, an American Indian Literary Magazine,* and discovered poems, stories, photographs, and artwork by dozens of talented Indian literary artists throughout the nation.

Indians, I believe Stegner correctly reasoned, could do best for themselves by writing their own novels, histories, short stories, poems, essays, articles, and literary criticism. They might even, God help us, eventually establish a voice for all of us in the West. Admittedly this was a radical way to think: that westerners can select—choose and manage—their own societies, that in order to have a literature at all, western writers—whether Native American or Anglo American, Chinese American or African American—need to tell their own particular stories rather than permit themselves and their cultures to be colonized (and therefore marginalized) by others. Without the telling of such particular stories, in fact, there can be no truly American literature.

The Native American past has been anything but marginalized in western American literature and history. On the contrary, too often it has taken center stage, most frequently and most regrettably as pulp fiction and romance. Non-Indian historians such as Dee Brown and Alvin Josephy, Jr., have made a profession out of western history told reasonably straight from an Indian point of view, just as non-Indian novelists such as Oliver La Farge, Frank Waters, and Tony Hillerman have made their reputations principally by writing "Indian" novels. The "Indian" past that La Farge and Waters create, however, is not *their* past. It is a past that belongs to the Navajos and the Pueblos. "This is one of the problems of having the archeology of the country not your own," Stegner commented to Milton. "One of the handicaps of being an interloper, and newcomer. I just don't think there is any real cure for that kind of thing until the residence of this particular culture has extended over a good many generations" (114).

Although rare, a book such as James Welch's *Killing Custer* (1994) is something else. It helps to have a Plains Indian—in this case a Blackfeet—to rethink the history of the Plains Indians, to demonstrate why winning the most famous battle in western American history proved so disastrous to its Native American victors. A writer such as Sherman Alexie, a self-styled member of the Brady Bunch Generation who can manipulate popular culture and turn prevaricated images of Indians against themselves, is also rare, for nobody has been more adversely affected by prevaricated images of themselves than Native Americans (and other marginalized groups): in the West, for instance, every other fry cook, bookkeeper, computer salesman, printer, and professor is still a "cowboy" or a "cowgirl," if only on the weekend. Although they are vastly outnumbered by federal and state employees, of course, there are also a few genuine working cowboys and cowgirls in the contemporary West, but they are damn few. Of the few I know, not a single one is characterized by the self-righteous, limited, racist, sexist, violent code that governs such mythic figures as the Virginian and Shane. Like Tonto, Shane and the Virginian are pan-American figures, as endemic to Chicago and New Jersey as they are to Los Angeles or Wyoming. By the same token, if the West we live in is, in Wallace Stegner's famous phrase, the "native home of hope," it is also the original home of the drive-by shooting. In "Variations on a Theme by Crèvecoeur," Stegner notes that Call and Gus, the two ex-Texas Rangers in his former student Larry McMurtry's Pulitzer Prizewinning novel *Lonesome Dove*, "kill more people than all the outlaws in that book put together do" (109). Their killings, however, are *righteous*.

Part of what attracted me to *Angle of Repose*, and one reason I was obsessed with its creation during our first and second interviews, is the novel's lack of violence. *Angle of Repose* begins where all those Hollywood horse operas end: with the civilizing woman, Susan Burling Ward, and the freedom-loving man, Oliver Ward, riding west into the sunset, locked in the holy but invisible chains of matrimony. Stories, I have always thought and still believe, are inherently useful, although just how often eludes us even while we are using them. In March of 1982, when I first visited the Stegners at their home, I was happily divorced but about to be married myself. Consequently, I can see now one more reason why I was intensely interested in Stegner's matrimonial case histories, both real and fictional. He and his wife, Mary, had been married for forty-five years. As a writer, one of the things I was also learning about *Angle of Repose* was that it can be read as metafiction, as a novel expressly concerned with the art of making stories, whether histories or novels. This is probably apparent to any reasonably intelligent reader, but it had yet to be pointed out in print, so I was also in the process of doing that by way of my dissertation when Stegner and I met to record the second formal interview this volume contains.

As a closet fiction writer and a scholar of Western American literature, I was also fascinated by Stegner's mastery of technique in *Angle of Repose*, particularly by his ability to employ, through the controlling intelligence of a first-person narrator, virtually every point of view known to exist, including stream of consciousness, first-person participant, first-person observer, second person, third-person omniscient, and third-person

limited. For me, *Angle of Repose* was a breakthrough novel
in terms of point of view, in its own way as important as
Joyce's *Ulysses*, although I could see that it was principally
from Faulkner and James, not Joyce, that Stegner had learned
to do what he was doing. So far as I could tell, not even John
Barth, Vladmir Nabokov, or John Fowles had exploited metafictional techniques as masterfully as Stegner had. He was
really, I concluded, playing the fashionable techniques of these
so-called "chaos-drunk" writers against themselves by sticking
to the "old fashioned" virtues of realism. Unlike Fowles in *The
French Lieutenant's Woman* or Nabokov in *Ada*, for example, in
Angle of Repose Stegner never drops (or pretends to lower) his
mask and directly address the reader. In other words, like a
good realist, Wallace Stegner never purposely lets his puppet
strings show or points to himself in the act of writing, although
his narrator, Lyman Ward, does so continually.

The metafictionists, by contrast, conformed to type: they
reveled in showing the reader not only their author's puppet
strings but also their hands and feet, in pointing out the stage
curtain as well as the set. Although I could never quite goad
him into saying so on tape, I think Wally thought writers such
as Barth and Nabokov were sometimes doing no more than
showing off their technical abilities in their metafictional
novels. I think he thought such novels were *all* technique,
just as he thought most "cowboys" (including Ronald Reagan)
were all big hat and no cattle. He wanted his metafictional
work to be something much more than a clever novel about
the art of writing novels. He wanted it to be a fictional garden
with real people in it. Most of all, I think he wanted to move
his readers emotionally *and* intellectually, to match up an
authentic western past with an equally authentic western
present. Accomplishing that would be the equivalent of doing
for the West what Faulkner had done for the South. Moreover,
it would be doing something that had never been done before,
or, at the very least, not the way he did it. For Stegner,
Hemingway was a man with a present but no past, whereas

Faulkner had them both. "This is what I'd really like to see some western writer manage to do," he had told John Milton: "put together his past and his present" (114).

"The house of fiction has not one window but a million," Henry James wrote in his famous preface to *A Portrait of a Lady* (1881). Ever since first reading *Angle of Repose* in about 1976, the phrase "house of fiction" has resonated within me like a tuning fork. Did I only imagine that the phrase resonated somewhere in Wallace Stegner's mind as well when he set his narrator, Lyman Ward, down in his house of fiction, "Zodiac Cottage," in the bonehouse of his imaginary body with its missing limb? The most characteristic figure in all of American literature is the American orphan. However he came by his names, whether consciously, as I tried to suggest in our second interview, or almost by chance, as Stegner implies, in the novel Lyman Ward functions *as* a ward, as both a literal and symbolic orphan, as well as a cultural guardian and gatekeeper. Like Charon, the river runner of the Greek underworld, Lyman Ward ferries souls back and forth between worlds. In our interviews, Stegner nevertheless denies making any conscious connections between his narrator's names and his functions.

Still, if we can generalize about anything, I believe that we can also safely say that in Stegner's fiction the West functions both literally and metaphorically as "America, only more so," the United States at its most rootless, energetic, culturally half-baked, politically reactionary end. In my dissertation I contended that by making Lyman Ward an amputee, Stegner was either consciously or unconsciously transplanting the hermetic grotesques of Hawthorne, Faulkner, and Flannery O'Connor from one end of the North American continent to the other. As our second interview indicates, however, I could never get him to admit publicly what he had done. Lyman's malaise —he suffers from partial paralysis, "tunnel vision," and a bone disease—obviously signals a cultural malaise as well. Like Lyman, most of us "want to touch the ground we have been maimed away from." Not all of us, however, are as lucky as

Lyman is to be able to mine the tailings of gifted ancestors in order to understand better who we are, but Lyman's luck is also Wallace Stegner's luck and our luck, too, if only by osmosis. Such luck is the reason we read, as Wallace Stegner pointed out long ago in an essay entitled "Fiction: A Lens on Life." "In all our wandering through real or fictional worlds," he writes, "it is probably ourselves we seek, and since that encounter is impossible we want the next-best thing: the completely intimate contact which may show us another like ourselves" (24).

At any rate, very few days in my life can compare with the exhilaration of spending the better part of a week at Casa Stegner during our final recorded talks at the beginning of January 1987. Not for the last time in their lives, Wallace and Mary Stegner were extraordinarily kind. All days should begin and end as those days did, up at 6:30 A.M. to breakfast then off for a few hours, either separately to write or together to talk books, then a break for the mail and the telephone and sometimes a run to the market. Lunch at noon with Mary. Afterwards, another two-hour recording session. Midafternoons we pushed the wheelbarrow and shoveled manure around recently planted lemon trees or stacked wood or took a walk. Late afternoons and evenings he always offered me the full use of his study. Sometimes I took advantage of the offer, sometimes not. I remember the two of us half-watching Arizona beat Stanford in basketball on the Stegners' twelve-inch black-and-white set. One evening we had a lively dinner with John and Marilyn Daniel, a young couple who rented the cottage below the house. Afterwards the five of us relaxed over drinks. It's no accident that a decade later the Daniels and the Gonzales-Hepworths are close friends. As with so many things, we have Wallace and Mary Stegner to thank for that.

Another evening Mary went off to a concert on campus. I was puzzled because he had declined for both of us Mary's persistent invitations to attend, and I had been interested in going before he told her we had "work" to do.

We ended up doing the dishes. He washed. I dried. As I
finished toweling the last pot, I asked, "Are we going to work
now?" By then I had already correctly guessed that he had no
intention of going back to the interviews or writing or even
reading. We were through for the day. He just hadn't wanted
to go to the concert, and he had used me as a convenient ex-
cuse to send Mary off with a friend. He looked down at me
with a wounded gaze, as if to say, along with William Stafford,
"There are so many things admirable people do not understand," but when I smiled, he smiled too. And then he
chuckled out loud.

Later, reading in bed behind the nearly closed door of the
guest room while Wally turned off the lights in the rest of the
house, I thought of an anecdote Nancy Colberg had related
to me. Apparently she and Mary had attended one of Wally's
formal lectures. Far into the talk, Mary turned to her com-
panion and whispered "Blah, blah, blah, blah, blah." It was
probably an apocryphal story, but I liked it not only because it
was humorous, but because in my mind it made an exemplary
couple more real.

Our last day together, however, began for me in emotional
darkness.

I was a pack-a-day smoker in 1987. The last morning of my
stay, at about 6:30—I had skipped breakfast but he had eaten,
and we had tiptoed out through the glass doors like a couple
of kids to let Mary "sleep in" until 7:30—I stood on the deck
smoking, meditatively, a cigarette that I had just lit, watching
the dim light filter and flare into day. Wally had gone inside his
study to light the kindling fire in the woodstove a few minutes
before. I had assumed he had gone in to write, and that I
might join him later. We had worked that way before, separately but in tandem, and we were both facing editorial dead-
lines. To my surprise he came back outside and stopped just a
few feet away; without glancing at me, he looked off in the
same general direction that I had been looking.

In my experience, smoking is among the most sociable

pastimes in the world, so much so that the confraternity of smokers needs no explanation. Still I felt awkward. Although they had both been cigarette smokers in their twenties and neither of them ever said anything about my smoking, I knew neither of them quite approved, either. Ten years had passed since the day we first met. Wally was now seventy-eight years old. I depended on him to give me sensible grandfatherly and even fatherly advice whenever I needed it, but I wasn't in the mood for taking any advice right now, and I kept feeling as if he was about to give me some. I hadn't slept much, and I was irritated at the world in general. I still had several chapters of my dissertation to write.

For whatever reasons, the two of us continued relaxing on the deck for ten minutes, watching the day come alive in the treetops just above and below us, silently thinking our separate thoughts, and for once I didn't say anything. Maybe there was no need to say anything. Maybe everything had been said. Maybe the work we were doing was useless and would come to nothing. After all, that's what usually happened with writing. On the other hand, it wasn't just me, Wally said, who wrote slowly. Sure, talent helps. But revision is what separates the men from the boys and the women from the girls, and writers could learn to revise. He said that 90 percent of what he wrote one day would sometimes have to be thrown away the next. With a few exceptions, it had been that way, he said, all his life, although the writing went even slower now because of his age. Still, he had said, writing, like marriage, is far less a product than a process. He had quoted Picasso: "I do not seek, I find." Right then, of course, he wasn't saying anything. He was just standing on the deck looking off into the distance.

It was also possible, I thought, that his novels might be too quiet, that his new book, which would not be out for several months yet, but which he had been good enough to let Tanya and me read in manuscript, was missing all the elements that define contemporary fiction, the very things that would make readers want to buy it. Just because Tanya and I had responded so powerfully to it didn't mean anyone else would. What if I was wrong? What if it wasn't one of his best?

Of all the quiet novels he wrote, *Crossing to Safety* is the quietest. There are no promiscuities, infidelities, divorces, and certainly no kinky sex scenes. Even *Angle of Repose* and *The Spectator Bird* obliquely include such things. True: the author never dramatizes them, but his narrators discuss those issues and refer to them. There are, for instance, Lyman's talks about novel writing and explicitly sexual matters with his attractive girl-Friday, Shelly Rasmussen, and in *The Spectator Bird* the narrator's flirtation with infidelity and the novel's theme of incest haunt us like specters. But in *Crossing to Safety*, as Larry Morgan, the narrator admits, "all the things that novelists seize upon and readers expect" appear to be missing. "Where," he asks, are the death wishes, "the suburban infidelities, the promiscuities, the convulsive divorces, the alcohol, the drugs, the lost weekends . . . the hatreds, the political ambitions, the lust for power . . . the speed, noise, ugliness, everything that makes us who we are and makes us recognize ourselves in fiction?" The two couples he writes about are not merely "hangovers from a quieter time. They have been able to buy quiet, and distance themselves from industrial ugliness" (195). That statement is surely more true for the wealthy couple, the Langs, than it is for the Morgans, but even the westerners, the Morgans, are protected by their intelligence and civilized tradition from "most of the temptations, indiscretions, vulgarities, and passionate errors that pester and perturb most of us" (195).

Plenty had changed in the five years between my last visit and this one, and as I continued smoking, I tried to imagine how many more changes the Stegners must have witnessed since building on this land in the 1940s and how it might have looked then. Where I was looking there had once been only rolling peninsula hillside. Now million-dollar houses, single-family dwellings, were being constructed on bare rises and the lion-colored hillsides terraced to accommodate them. By contrast with the Stegners' well-designed but modest two-bedroom home, the houses across the way appeared vulgar to me. He and Mary surely must have resented them. Charity Lang's "dreamhouse" in *Crossing to Safety* would be small, I thought, compared to some of those monstrosities. In the first light of the morning, I could already hear a loud pop from a piece of heavy equipment. The sound of the engine after it caught was mercifully muted by distance and the otherwise somber quiet of the early morning. Then the muffled sound of the engine died altogether, and the bird choir took over again.

As I went on smoking and thinking, I kept stealing glances at Wally and wondering if *he* had crossed to safety yet and, if he had, whether or not he had reached any sort of repose, angled or otherwise. It seemed to me that he had, and that he had reached it long ago, certainly by the time we had met. He still didn't look his age, though. How had he done it all? How could any one person possibly have balanced so many responsibilities—marriage, family, teaching, public service, writing—and excelled to such a degree at everything he did?

I knew part of what fascinated me about both him and Mary was their decency, their graciousness, their compassion and understanding, but I was also fascinated by their sheer talent. Wally didn't just write novels. He wrote short stories, novels, biographies, essays, literary criticism, and history. Mary didn't know just a little bit about editing. She knew a lot about editing. And music. And art. However much they might have baffled others, in my eyes they were an ideal couple, highly cultivated and well-meaning, but I had never been quite sure what to do with their generosity—or how to repay it. Wally was always loaning or giving me books through the mail. So I sent him some of the books I published. Mary wrote us her own notes and letters. So we wrote her back. She called Tanya and me regularly, if not frequently, to check up on us. I especially remember being reassured by the sound of her voice after our triplets were stillborn. She had also called after each of our son, Myrlin's, two open-heart surgeries.

Myrlin, in fact, had just undergone his second surgery before I flew off to conduct these last interviews. How was I going to pay off *that* debt, which, I had learned on the phone only last night, had now ballooned into six figures? Was that what was bothering me? Money? Debt?

Crossing to Safety was, for Tanya and me, all the more special a book because it was about a rare kind of friendship —a friendship between couples—the kind of friendship the Stegners had shown us ever since we had been married in Santa Fe in 1982. On the other hand, Tanya and I also knew perfectly well by now that we were no special phenomenon. Wally and Mary had extended the same brand of kindness to so many couples over the years that it was second nature to them. We hadn't earned it, we didn't deserve it, and it couldn't last. But while it did we always felt like two of the chosen.

Of course we also knew Wallace Stegner was going to die. So did everyone else, including Wally. He was nearing eighty years old. I wanted to ask him what he thought about death and dying, but I didn't know if I had either the right or the courage. I was pretty sure I would never be prepared for his death no matter when it happened.

"I'm not even sure if I quite know what evil is," he had told John Milton once, "but I suspect, among other things it's ignorance, sometimes maybe even malevolence, outright malevolence" (113). I'm not sure evil exists in his books, either, any more than it did in his life. In *Crossing to Safety*, Larry's dismissal from the university does not even strike him, given the circumstances of the Depression, as particularly unfair. Likewise the mangled hand of the Italian construction worker is an abhorrent wound, but it qualifies merely as an accident, not as evil. Even the onset of Sally's polio is put down to brute chance and somehow ameliorated and therefore lived with and endured. Only Charity's death and dying comes at all close to what we usually mean by the word *evil*. As I stood on the deck that morning smoking my cigarette in silence and wondering how I was ever going to pay off my debts, I began to see that

Crossing to Safety is a novel about confronting death, and accepting it, and learning from it.

From scrupulously mining Richard Etulain's *Conversations* and unscrupulously asking pointed questions off the record, I knew that the couples in the novel were based on the Stegners and their friends, Philip and Peg Grey, but although *Crossing to Safety* was perhaps his most autobiographical novel since *The Big Rock Candy Mountain*, I also knew enough not to push comparisons too hard. It *was* a novel, after all, not a memoir. Above all I also knew that I owed Wallace Stegner an unpayable debt. "Friends don't *have* to repay anything," Charity tells Sally and Larry in *Crossing to Safety*, when they accept the Langs' offer to take Sally and the baby to Vermont's Battell Pond for the summer and leave Larry the run of their Madison house while he teaches summer school. "Friendship is the most selfish thing there is."

"It's been good to have you here," Wally said to me without prompting. "I'm glad you came, that we got this chance together."

Suddenly, the silence on the deck had been broken, and without knowing it, I had just extinguished my cigarette. "Thanks for having me," I ventured, turning toward him.

"You're welcome any time," he shot back. "It's been our pleasure."

I tried to look at him to better gauge the remark, but he was already smiling again. Besides, it was typical of him to insist that the Stegner generosity was selfish and to convince you that he meant it.

"Shall we go inside?" he said, but it wasn't really a question. He was already leading the way.

I refer my actions to his standards even yet. Sure, there were going to be other times to share together in the next six years before he died. But I returned to the house only infrequently after that morning, never for more than a day and usually for just part of an afternoon or an evening, and always in the company of others. He and Mary, for instance, hosted a publication party at their house for Nancy Colberg's descriptive bibliography on the day I published it. Book collectors and dealers came from as far away as Los Angeles and Colorado, and we all stayed well past midnight. There were providential meetings, too, like the one when he and Mary came to Oregon to present his "ruminations" on the art of fiction for the Portland Arts and Lectures Series. But when all is said and done, and I have to choose where to leave the two of us, I put us out on that deck at sunrise with Wally smiling and leading the way toward the study.

If, as I believe, he succeeded in *Crossing to Safety* in doing what novelists are supposed to do, if he did, in fact, "create a world," then it is a world of love, which must include death and suffer it and vanquish it. The novel is nothing if not a proof of grief and love's victory over death.

I believe he and Mary knew how Tanya and I felt about them, how we all felt about them. I hope they did. We loved them. But just in case they didn't, I use their kindness and their own words to tell them now.

WORKS CONSULTED

Arthur, Anthony, ed. *Critical Essays on Wallace Stegner.*
Boston: G. K. Hall, 1982.

Barth, John. "The Literature of Exhaustion." *The Atlantic* 220 (1967): 2934.

Benson, Jackson J. *Wallace Stegner: His Life and Work.* New York: Viking, 1996.

Berry, Wendell. "Wallace Stegner and the Great Community."
South Dakota Review 23 (4) (1985): 10-18.

Colberg, Nancy. *Wallace Stegner: A Descriptive Bibliography.*
Lewiston, Idaho: Confluence Press, 1990.

Etulain, Richard. *Conversations with Wallace Stegner on Western History and Literature.* Salt Lake City: University of Utah Press, 1983.

Fowles, *The French Lieutenant's Woman.* Boston: Little, Brown, 1969.

James, Henry. *The Portrait of a Lady.* Ed. by Robert D. Bramberg.
New York: W.W. Norton, 1975.

Joyce, James. *Ulysses.* New York: Random House, 1961.

McMurtry, Larry. *Lonesome Dove*. New York: Simon and Schuster, 1985.

Meine, Curt. *Wallace Stegner and the Continental Vision: Essays on Literature, History, and Landscape*. Washington, DC: Island Press, 1997.

Milton, John. "Conversation with Wallace Stegner." *South Dakota Review* 23(4) (1985): 10718.

Miller, Mark Crispin. "The Crushing Power of Big Publishing." *The Nation* 264(10) (1997): 1118.

Nabokov, Vladmir V. *Ada, or Ardor, A Family Chronicle*. New York: McGraw-Hill, 1969.

Robinson, Forest G., and Margaret G. Robinson. *Wallace Stegner*. Boston: G. K. Hall, 1977.

Schoff, Gretchen Holstein. "Where the Blue Sings." *The Geography of Hope*. San Francisco: Sierra Club Books, 1996.

Stegner, Page, ed. "Preface." *The Geography of Hope*. Page Stegner and Mary Stegner, eds. San Francisco: Sierra Club Books, 1996..

Stegner, Wallace. *All the Little Live Things*. New York: Viking, 1967.

———. *American Places*. With Page Stegner and Eliot Porter. New York: Greenwich House, 1981.

———. *The American West as Living Space*. Ann Arbor: University of Michigan Press, 1987.

———. *Angle of Repose*. Garden City, NY: Doubleday, 1971.

———. *The Big Rock Candy Mountain*. New York: Duell, Sloan, and Pearce, 1943.

———. *Collected Stories*. New York: Random House, 1990.

———. *Crossing to Safety*. New York: Random House, 1987.

———. *Fire and Ice*. New York: Duell, Sloan, and Pearce, 1941.

———. "Fiction: A Lens on Life." *One Way to Spell Man: Essays with a Western Bias*. Garden City, N.Y.: Doubleday, 1982.

———. "Foreword" to *The Uncommon Touch: Fiction and Poetry from the Stanford Writing Workshop*. Ed. by John L'Heureux. Palo Alto, CA: Stanford University Press, 1989.

———. *The Gathering of Zion: The Story of the Mormon Trail*. New York: McGraw-Hill, 1964.

———. *Mormon Country*. New York: Duell, Sloan, and Pearce, 1942.

———. *On a Darkling Plain*. New York: Harcourt, Brace, 1940.

———. *One Way to Spell Man: Essays with a Western Bias.* Garden City, N.Y.: Doubleday, 1982.

———. *The Potter's House.* Muscatine: Prairie Press, 1938.

———. *Recapitulation.* Garden City, NY: Doubleday, 1979.

———. *The Sound of Mountain Water.* Garden City, N.Y.: Doubleday, 1969.

———. *The Spectator Bird.* Garden City, NY: Doubleday, 1976.

———. *20-20 Vision: In Celebration of the Peninsula Hills.* Palo Alto, CA: Green Foothills Foundation, 1982.

———. *The Uneasy Chair: A Biography of Bernard DeVoto.* Garden City, NY: Doubleday, 1974.

———. "Variations on a Theme by Crèvecoeur." *The American West as Living Space.* Ann Arbor: University of Michigan Press, 1987.

———. *Where the Blue Bird Sings to the Lemonade Springs: Living and Writing in the West.* New York: Random House, 1992.

Welch, James, with Paul Steckler. *Killing Custer.* New York: W.W. Norton, 1994.

West, Elliott. "Stegner, Storytelling, and Western Identity." *Wallace Stegner: Man & Writer.* Ed. by Charles Rankin. Albuquerque: University of New Mexico Press, 1996.

14 APRIL 1977
Tucson, Arizona

Interviewer: I grew up with a book of your essays entitled The
Sound of Mountain Water. *In that book you said something
that as an adolescent writer living in southern Idaho I very much
wanted to hear. You claimed that a publisher's map of the United
States would look like a barbell: New York at one end, California
at the other, and in between, United Air Lines. Do you think that
comparison still holds true?*

Stegner: In some ways, yes. It is perfectly plain that publishers
know the West Coast exists. I think they are less certain about
the interior parts of the country. They do know, I suppose,
even some of the major issues in a kind of New York or
Boston way, misunderstanding what's going on in the West
with the best will in the world. I'm afraid there is something
that happens between Thirty-third Street and about Sixty-fifth
and then between Third Avenue and Avenue of the Americas
that is essentially the publishing world, and it's a very narrow
world. The horizons don't spread very wide. People who don't
run in that pasture are less likely to seem part of the world.
This is true whether you live in Iowa City or Tucson or San
Francisco or anywhere else. The publishing world is New
York, even to editors who come from outside and who should
know better, who do have roots in some other kind of world.
I can't think of any cure for that except to disperse the publishing business beyond the Urals and scatter it around a little bit.
This might make it less convenient to have lunch with a client, | 29

but I think some regional centers for publishing would be
useful —if they didn't get too addicted to themselves and
become mutual admiration societies for another little circle
of a regional kind.

I think the narrow view applies in many other ways, too,
to things that don't have so much to do with the publishing
of books, but do have to do with the merchandising of books,
and the notice of books. For instance, I've been griping for the
last month about the merchandising methods of wholesalers,
because books are all being put on computers now, and everybody runs through a little system which puts you up against
some publication profile. If you don't fit into the profile, your
book is probably not a book that they think they should publish. Publishers get timid, like Hollywood moviemakers, trying
to reproduce successes only and never taking chances.

*Interviewer: You mean they put the
profile of the writer onto a computer?*

Stegner: They put his book in the profile of their publishing,
and if it isn't a subject matter or a kind of book they think
they have had luck with or would have luck with, then it's
rejected. Wholesalers have their headquarters, say, in Nashville,
Tennessee, or some such place, and the computer feedouts that
come from there are what bookstores all over the country are
given to buy from, with the result that if the book is not on
the computer printout, the bookstore owner, unless he's sharp,
never even hears of it. That printout that comes out of the
merchandiser's is an eastern printout.

I mean, these are books that Nashville is interested in,
or certainly San Francisco, so if you run a bookstore in San
Francisco or Canyon City, Colorado, you had better not
depend on the printout, and I know a lot of booksellers who
are very angry at what they get to buy. They don't get any
salesmanship on any books except those on the printout.
That's a long answer to a perfectly straightforward question,

but I do think that communications are not so good that we can depend on New York to look to the interests of the whole country. The whole country looks different from New York.

Interviewer: In the past, writers from the West, men like Bernard DeVoto and others including yourself who might be said to represent a western point of view, found it necessary to literally move east in order to break into serious print. Certainly, this is less true of you than of DeVoto, and today we even have poets like Richard Hugo who have ongoing contracts with publishers like Norton, writers who can afford to live out here and still be published and read. Is it still necessary for a young writer to move east in order to be marketed, in order to be taken seriously?

Stegner: I think it's pretty difficult if you don't spend a lot of time in New York, if you don't have the personal contacts and go to the lunches at the Algonquin or whatever. I taught at Harvard for a half-dozen years, and I have the pronounced feeling that then—which is nearly forty years ago now—I was much more in the literary world than I am now. That's because I've lived on the West Coast for the last thirty-odd years and haven't gone east much. I have gone east only when I couldn't help it. That's actually asking for it.

That's like pulling the blanket over your head in a Squaw Dance. You're not going to be recognized if you don't stick your face out. If you want to do it that way, well, all right, but most people feel that they have to go east now and again. I should go east for the National Institute meetings, for instance.

Interviewer: You should have been there for the National Book Awards yesterday, too, since you were one of the winners.

Stegner: I was just as glad to be here, but let me return to your question. The distance between writer and publisher is simply too great for the writer to be borne in mind unless he keeps reminding people of himself. It's like the old formula for a radio play, a thing that doesn't exist anymore. When Archie MacLeish and people like that were writing radio plays, there was a kind of rule that you couldn't let a character in a radio play *not* speak for more than sixty seconds. If you let him go for longer than that, he'd disappear from the play, because there's no way of reminding the audience he's there except by his voice. It's all you have to go with. You have a little of that when you're working from a remote place, even San Francisco, which is a much more strategic place to work from than, say, Tucson or Salt Lake City or anywhere in the interior.

Interviewer: When you say be seen, *be seen by whom? By a publisher?*

Stegner: Be seen by—Oh, I don't know—walk by Random House and run into Red Warren. Just be around New York. You don't disappear then.

Interviewer: But if you have a good agent and a good house and you trust them to stand behind your work, do you still need that?

Stegner: We were talking about this earlier in the morning. I think you probably don't need it. You can work by mail, but it's far less certain, partly because—inevitably—and it would happen in reverse if the circumstances were reversed—cliques form. New York book reviewers write competitively against one another and for one another's eyes. This was somewhat truer when the book review media were themselves more competitive. There's only one now, maybe two, or one and a half. It's unlikely that you will get to review or be reviewed if you're outside those cliques, unless, of course, you can simply make enough noise that you can impose yourself on them, but a first, a second, a third novel is likely to disappear off their canvas.

Interviewer: Yes. Norman McCleod's work stands as a classic example, or rather, it doesn't stand, because it's out of print.

Stegner: I know that name, but I'm not sure
I've ever read any of his work.

Interviewer: Well, as a young poet, he was probably better translated into other languages than either Eliot or Pound, but today his name is relatively unknown. The man also wrote two novels, both of which I believe received some critical attention, but then he was shelved, partly because of personal circumstances, partly because his work is set in the West, but partly because he simply moved out of that pasture you mentioned earlier, away from New York.

Stegner: You mean you think there are some mute inglorious
Miltons? Well, there well may be. I always used to have faith
that if a book was good enough it would find, in the first place,
a publisher, and, in the second place, a certain body of readers,
probably not as many as if it were in the places where fashion
is made. I still, I guess, with some reservations, believe that.
If you write well enough, you'll find a publisher who will be
happy to publish you, even if he doesn't make much money
out of you, but the audience does bother me, I must admit,
because it seems to me that failure to find an audience is not
the publisher's fault: it's primarily the fault of the wholesale
bookseller, and, to some extent the fault of the book review
media, which, by now are too few and too noncompetitive
to do the job. It's often done by cliques, as I mentioned, and
sometimes by people who shouldn't be reviewing books at all,
who shouldn't be allowed within arm's length of a book.

I sound fierce and disgruntled, but I think the path of talent
from the provinces is a harder path than it used to be, and it's
harder than it ought to be. Just as a sample: five minutes ago
—and this is entirely because of the National Book Award
—Norman Cousins called me up and asked me to go to Russia

with a delegation of American writers. He wouldn't have
called me unless the accident of the Book Award had happened,
in spite of the fact that I used to be a kind of contributing
editor of *The Saturday Review.*

Interviewer: Did you accept? Are you going?

Stegner: No, I don't think so.

Interviewer: Whatever happened to your work with Saturday Review
and Atlantic*? I don't see your short work in the magazines anymore.*

Stegner: I haven't done much magazine work lately. That's
partly because I'm getting old, and it's partly because I quit
teaching. Short things you can do while you're teaching.
With long ones, it's harder. And also, I think short stories are
a young man's racket. I haven't written one for fifteen years.
Essays? I suppose I have less brash confidence that I have anything to say to anyone in an informational or personal essay
way, and so I don't write them often.

*Interviewer: There's some talk circulating now that says the idea of
conservation is primarily a child of the West. Certainly a great many
writers from the West have been ardent conservationists, including you
and Bernard DeVoto.*

Stegner: Some of the most effective organizations came out of
the West, and that's partly a function of the fact that the West is
opener and newer and less industrialized and spoiled than some
other parts of the country. The Wilderness Society really came
out of Moose, Wyoming. The Sierra Club's headquarters has
always been in Berkeley or San Francisco. These are originally
western organizations. I don't know where the Izaak Walton
League was formed. Denver, wasn't it? In any case, I think it,
too, originated in the West. Those are three of the most
important conservation groups, and they are the ones who

have, over a period now of nearly a generation, built it from
a little nest of enthusiasts into something like a broad-based
movement, until the Whole Earth years and a lot of uprising
of the sixties joined the movement. I suppose if it weren't
for a lot of angry young people in Montana at the moment,
Montana would be down the drain, down the coal slurry tube.
But conservation hasn't remained strictly western. The two
states that have the best environmental laws that I know of are
Oregon, on the one hand, and Vermont on the other.

*Interviewer: In one of your essays you say that Vermont reminds you
more of the West you knew as a young man than the present-day
West itself does.*

Stegner: Well, northeastern Vermont is
still wild woods, you know.

*Interviewer: But they're deciduous woods as
opposed to the coniferous woods of the West.*

Stegner: I wasn't thinking of leafage. I was thinking, too, of our
part of Vermont, which is right under the Canadian line. Even
where there were farms in the 1860s, everybody went off to
the war or the gold rush or something and left all the women
behind, and the women died off or went down country. A lot
of those farms have gone back to wilderness. My old farm in
Vermont is really full of bears and wildcats. I can't go out in
the raspberry patch without running across smoking bear dung.
It makes me look over my shoulder. Vermont is also a hunter's
country. Every farmer around there is a hunter. They have the
same (to me) insane views about the right to own and carry
firearms that the West has always had, that I grew up with. I
disagree with that, but it reminds me of the West. So it goes.
And these people are very hardy outdoor people with an awful
lot of frontier knacks, Yankee ingenuity, plus the fact that they
live on shoestrings and make half of what they use and can

repair anything and live off porcupine quills if they have to.
The dialect, and, as you say, the leafery, are not Western, but
a lot of other things are. It's a good place. You come up and
I'll show you, convince you. And it's not all deciduous anyway. It's what they call a mixed northern forest with a lot of
hemlock, larch, white pine, balsam fir, and so on, all mixed.

*Interviewer: I've never really gotten the biography
and geography of your early years straight.*

Stegner: My first memories are of Seattle, sitting on the back
step of a tenement house and telling the kid next door, "I'm
half Indian and half Jew, but don't tell anybody."

Interviewer: Are you?

Stegner: No, but it made a good story. Then we went to
Saskatchewan to make a million dollars out of wheat along
that short grass frontier that should never have been plowed.
So we made our dust bowl and burned out along with everybody else, and then we wound up in Montana, and from
Montana drifted down to Salt Lake. By that time my father
was chasing mining claims.

Interviewer: Much of that appears in Big Rock Candy Mountain.
How much of Angle of Repose *is fact, or history?*

Stegner: Angle of Repose? I couldn't tell you. It's based, obviously,
on the papers of Mary Hallock Foote. I used her as a model,
but whenever her papers didn't suit me, I changed them,
which is why it is a novel and not a biography. If I'd been
writing her biography, I couldn't have changed them. When
I wanted to do something to her life which never happened
—she lived to be ninety-five years old and died happily in the
bosom of her family revered by a large and loving clan—I gave

her some hard times she didn't have in order to make a novel out of it. I seem to be place-conscious. In *Big Rock Candy Mountain,* I used the places where we had lived. In *Angle of Repose,* I used the places where this family actually lived, because it is easier to write about places I know and have a lot of documentation on.

Interviewer: Did you go back to the actual places, say, to Boise and to Arrow Rock Dam? Where did you do the actual writing?

Stegner: I'd been through Boise a couple of times, but I've never seen Arrow Rock Dam. I've never been over Mosquito Pass, either. But I have seen a lot of mountain rivers, and I've been over lots of passes twelve thousand feet or more. If you describe one pass that you've been over, everybody who's been over Mosquito Pass will think it is Mosquito Pass. That's called faking it. I didn't have time to visit every place. I would have loved to go to the Colorado Rockies and fooled around. I had, of course, been to Leadville quite a lot, and I had been to Boise, and I knew the general lay of the land in both places, but I didn't bother to go up to the dam because, for one thing, I had some letters from the family I was dealing with that gave me a kind of clue to how it seemed then. I must have felt that to go and see it now would only confuse the picture I'd formed of it from reading the letters, and there's no reason to confuse the picture just to get a few facts. The facts aren't important except as they make the picture.

Interviewer: How many other novelists from the West have won the Pulitzer?

Stegner: Oh, I think quite a few. Bud Guthrie won it for *Big Sky.* H. L. Davis for *Honey and the Horn.* I think Paul Horgan must have won the Pulitzer Prize. I know that Oliver La Farge did with *Laughing Boy.*

Interviewer: I've always wondered how to define a western writer. How do you know if somebody is a western writer or not?

Stegner: Would you call Mark Twain a western writer? Is *Roughing It* a western book?

Interviewer: I'd say so, yes.

Stegner: Well, he was transplanted, you know. He hadn't even been here very long. Somebody like Jack Schaefer, who is the dean of all the shoot-them-up westerns, wasn't born in the West. He was born in the East, a long way east. In fact, Billy the Kid was not a westerner, either. I'm not sure what a westerner is. We get into these attitudes that somehow we're like plants, and we have something organic in us, and if we grow up in the sand, we eventually develop the right genes, and our seeds know when not to sprout, and something organic has happened. I'm not sure it's quite that organic, and I know a lot of people who were not born in the West, but have written good western books. They know the West at least as well as anybody here and better than most people born here. For instance, there's a lady here in town that I met last night, Frances Gillmor, who's written quite a lot. She comes from New Brunswick, Canada. The West isn't old enough to have very many native writers.

Interviewer: You once said that someone needs to do for the West what Faulkner did for the South.

Stegner: It would be nice.

Interviewer: What do you mean?

Stegner: You're thinking of a particular essay, I guess, in which I was complaining a little bit that western writers seem to suffer from a kind of disease that afflicted a lot of early American writers, too. Hawthorne, for example, felt the lack of a *usable past*, as he called it, and so was deliberately writing historical short stories and so on, deliberately mining the past he felt behind him and wanted to make use of. Henry James had the same kind of feeling that there was no society, no continuity, no court, no aristocracy, no anything that you could make novels out of, and he quoted Hawthorne very approvingly on the kind of thinness that a novelist had by way of materials in the United States. I think western writers have always felt that thinness, and one of the evidences of it is that almost all of us, in one way or another, have been lured off into history, trying to do exactly what Hawthorne was doing: to create a usable past. But creating a usable past in the West is confusing, because the history that passes for history isn't history at all, but myth, the Diamond Dick kind of stuff, which, as dime novel, and, later, as movie and as television serial and as pulp story, is absolutely foolproof, apparently. It will go on forever. But it confuses history. If you want to build a usable past, you almost have to cut that off. I have to take the scissors and separate myself from Jack Schaefer if I'm trying to write about a West that I think is real, not mythical.

Interviewer: Well, doesn't that account for some of the prejudice you were talking about earlier, particularly among the wholesale booksellers and publishers?

Stegner: I think it probably does, because they don't know there are two kind of western history, one real history and one artificial. Prejudice? I don't know whether it is prejudice or not. I had a kind of funny experience a year or two ago when I was in Italy. I got a call from a lady who was working for the outfit that makes Sesame Street television movies. She wanted me to meet Robert Redford about a thing he wanted to do. Redford married a Mormon girl, as you probably know, and he lives in Provo Canyon when he's home, and the Mormons are very interested in history. They're one part of the West that is very

history-conscious, and Redford got hipped on the real things
that had happened in the West instead of the old Jeremiah
Johnson kind of things he'd been playing in the films. The
phone call never did come to anything, but it did lead Redford
into doing a piece on the Kaiperowits Plateau and those coal-
fired power plants that they were planning to put in, which
killed them. I mean, he went out like the Lone Ranger with
two guns and he shot down these power plants, which was
dandy as far as I was concerned. Then I caught him the other
night on television being the narrator of a documentary on
wolves in the Yukon. Evidently Redford has learned the
difference between the real and the phony West. He's now
really interested in doing something serious about the real
West. I wish more people would.

*Interviewer: The movie you alluded to was
based on Vardis Fisher's book, wasn't it?*

Stegner: Well, yes, but they stole it, of course. They didn't get
permission to use it. Opal Fisher sued them and got something
out of them, but she doesn't think she got enough. They assumed
that Jeremiah Johnson was in the public domain because he
was a mountain man, and Fisher was writing something like
history, but they stayed a little too close to Fisher's book.

Interviewer: What do you think of Fisher's work?

Stegner: That's a little hard to answer because he was my freshman English teacher at the University of Utah. He was the first
writer I ever saw, and I thought his early novels—which Benny
DeVoto described as "the most unbuttoned fiction of our time"
—and I thought they were great. By the time he got around to
The Children of God, the one about the Mormon Migration. I
tried to read that one to my wife while I was writing *The Big
Rock Candy Mountain*. We were wintering in Vermont, snowed
in, no television, no radio; we read a lot, and I tried reading

that one aloud, and it just won't read. It's bad prose. Also I
think it's full of a kind of exaggeration, a kind of bluntness
of perception, that troubled me. I had thought Fisher was
better than that. And he may be. It may be just that book.
That's the one, of course, that DeVoto thought was so great,
and he ate crow publicly some place or other in a review saying,
"I thought Fisher was terrible, but this proves to me he's
good." I think what Benny was saying is that the Mormon
story is a terrific story.

*Interviewer: Whether it be southern writers, southwestern writers,
or western writers, I think publishers want stories that they know.*

Stegner: Sure, and it would take somebody good as Faulkner to
do for the West what he did for the South. But remember that
when Malcom Cowley finally wrote that introduction to the
portable Faulkner, and classified the Yoknapatawpha saga, every
book of Faulkner's was out of print. Faulkner used to annually
publish his book and take a beating. *The New Yorker* couldn't
have had more fun: "*Sound and the Fury!* Ha-Ha-Ha!" Clifton
Fadiman used to have his own ball game kicking Faulkner
around. It was the French, probably, not the Americans, who
made Faulkner a Nobel Prize winner. In any event, Faulkner
never got a good press in this country until Cowley took him
on and sorted out the Yoknapatawpha County saga, put its
parts in place. Faulkner himself admits as much in his letters.
He and Cowley had to adjust some things, rewrite the books
a little in order to make them match, and they don't quite
match yet. I know exactly how that goes because I'm stealing
a couple of my own short stories to put in the new novel, and I
can't quite make them match. In any case, Faulkner was a new
voice with new things to say and a new South to talk about, an
old one and a new one that derived out of the old one but was
quite different. Faulkner didn't impose it upon the American
reading public overnight. It took him a lifetime of work, and
it took a very perceptive critic, Cowley, to finally get him over

the hump. Within just a few years, he was practically an industry. Graduate schools were pouring out dissertations on him. I must have directed seven or eight myself.

Robert Houston: The problem now, though, is that if you don't write like Faulkner . . . if your characters don't beat blacks, hunt coons, aren't darkly tragic or slightly gothic . . . .

Stegner: You've got enough storytellers in the South, though. This is a place that is relatively rich in storytellers. The West is not. We can't forget southern writers like Walker Percy, Flannery O'Connor, Carson McCullers, Eudora Welty, and the others. They have some things in common, but they are definitely different voices.

Interviewer: You draw several parallels between southern fiction and the fiction of the real American West yourself.

Stegner: Well, the South had peanuts and the West had sugar beets. We were both in the same fix, a kind of provincial bag. Sure, there are parallels, except that we are way behind them, and I don't suppose, the way the West has developed, that we are ever going to develop in any way similar to the South. That was a kind of uniform climate, a uniform rural tradition made more self-conscious by defeat and by the whole slavery curse, with the result that it's a single thing with an enormous pressure underneath to get something said. Traditional to a degree. And I think the West is exactly what Walter Webb called it: *an oasis civilization,* a semi-arid country with a desert heart. People in the West are not fixed in the same way as the Sartorises and so on in Faulkner's towns, driving their old Queenie around the courthouse. We're absolutely mobile. This is the most migrant part of the United States, which probably means of the world. That isn't the way in which traditions get set up, a society out of which you can write novels. What comes out of it is likely to be very peripatetic. Kerouac's *On the Road* is a kind of inevitable—it seems to me—western novel. It also happens to match the spirit of the times, and you get that peripatetic saint, if indeed he is a saint.

But the mobility is characteristically western. I know guys in Minneapolis who dry-farm in Southern Saskatchewan and park their pickups, lease their equipment, or pick it up from wherever they left it, put in their crop, live there in their trailer or their pickup for three or four months, harvest their crop, and go back to Minneapolis. They are suitcase farmers. There's no society in it. Their society is Minneapolis, so you couldn't say they have done anything to Saskatchewan. There's no tradition except for their own mobility, which is just like an antelope's. They move for the same reasons the antelope do.

Interviewer: In one of the books I mentioned earlier, The Sound of Mountain Water, *you predicted that new boomtowns would spring up in the West, and that's exactly what has happened.*

Stegner: It didn't take a prophet to say that, because this country has never been settled, it's been raided, and whenever there is something to raid for there will be new raiders. Tucson is being raided, I suppose. It's part of the sunbelt, and certainly parts of California are being raided in the same way. It is very hard for any kind of community—which is one of the nicest things a novelist can have—when everything turns over on about a four-year basis.

Interviewer: Yesterday you mentioned a book called Zen and the Art of Motorcycle Maintenance. *I'm curious to know what you think about the incorporation of traditional thought of the Far East into current American thought.*

Stegner: Well, I don't know. It's not my bag. There's one thing that does strike me about the writing of fiction and probably of poetry, too, though I won't guarantee that. Literature is what the behavioral scientists call "hopelessly culture bound."

You work with the language, and the language itself is a terribly limiting—or enlarging—instrument. If you happen to be writing in Bengali and you don't have any past perfect tense in Bengali, you're kind of limited. It's not a good literary language, some languages are like that. They don't have the flexibility in their verbs, they don't have the kind of richness of vocabulary—whatever. English is a marvelous language, and I'm happy to be culture-bound in English, but I suppose I grew up completely in the Judeo-Christian tradition, and I never had any particular exposure to Zen or any of the other traditions.

What's happening is that the culture is changing, and when the culture changes, this will inevitably be reflected in the fiction. Maybe the fiction will have some part in changing the culture. I don't know our culture *can't* contain those things. It's absolutely open, and there are plenty of people spending their time studying Zen and other traditions. Gary Snyder is a good case in point. I suppose Gary Snyder makes Zen and Old Coyote and other kinds of people come together in a reasonable way. On the other hand, it can go to the point of absurdity, too, and you can get the Moonies incorporating their thing into the culture. I think that just has to be worn out and thrown away.

No, there's no reason on earth why a great religion shouldn't be a part of the consciousness of any world citizen, and I would hope that any western writer is as much a world citizen as any Romanian writer or any New York writer or anyone else. If he is aware of all those things, then he probably has a lot of questions and contradictions going on in his mind that have to be resolved. That's a very healthy situation for a writer. Questions ought to be going on. I'm not particularly religious and I don't follow the left-hand path. But I do believe in asking more questions than you can answer, and that's what a lot of people have been doing. A lot of the environmental movement that you've been talking about, and a lot of the peace movement, has been related to the passivism of Zen, and those things do

seem to match things in the Western world that are important
to an awful lot of people, including me. If I knew anything
about them, I would probably write in that vein.

*Interviewer: Yes. One thing I see happening now is that
the increasing changes are making the planet smaller.*

Stegner: Yes. We were all pretty much lost in Western civilization even as much as a generation ago. The kinds of things
one got an education in didn't even take into account half of
the world. The world has gotten smaller, and we must take
account of it. Certainly, to be culture-bound in this present
world is to be culture-bound within wider boundaries than if
you were Jane Austen, let us say, born in eighteenth-century
England. But I still think we're culture-bound. I still think that
the language inevitably steers us in ways we can't do anything
about—and probably shouldn't. The Western habit of taking
charge of one's environment and doing things to it and fixing
it is very much under challenge and attack. That's partly due
to environmentalism, it's partly due to notions learned from
the American Indians, and it's partly due to the quietism of
Zen and other eastern religions. I'm all for it, because I don't
believe in setting bulldozers loose in the earth.

There used to be an old joke, you know, about the old Hindu
who had a hole in front of his hut. He came out everyday and
walked around the hole. Some Peace Corps guy came and
lived in the hut with the Hindu and on the first day the Peace
Corps guy filled the hole up.

Perhaps that's the difference between an Eastern and Western attitude. You accept the fact in the first case. In the second,
you do something about it, but the moment you start doing
something about it—and I think the Greeks started that way
of dealing with the environment—you have to set limits or
you ultimately destroy the earth. It's too damned ingenious a
race. It's a weed species with great ingenuity. So I would stop
short of manhandling continents, and that means, I suppose,

admitting certain kinds of passivism, certain kinds of almost pantheism. [American] Indian attitudes toward the earth seem to me healthier than white attitudes, by and large.

Interviewer: When you write, do you write intuitively or are you conscious of any particular form?

Stegner: Oh, I know whether I'm writing a novel or a sonnet, yeah. I don't know about being conscious of form in another sense. There's a depth of concentration that you get into, and it may take you three hours to get into it, and you may write only an hour out of the daily four, but when you're in that kind of concentration, I don't think your critical awareness is alive at all. You're submerged. You're writing *out* of something. You're not standing outside and judging at that point. It's when you read it over the next morning that you judge it. I think when you're actually writing you're not being very critical. You have to incorporate a critic, but he comes in at a different hour. What guides you when you're actually getting some words on paper, I suppose, are things in the story itself, inevitabilities of character, confrontations of character, or the development of some kind of theme, or making pictures, or whatever it is you're doing. Those are the things that are important, and you do them any way you can. I do that over and over again. I rewrite every page in different ways, many times, not to make it satisfy any preconceived notion, but only because I still feel it isn't right. It's a little bit like smoothing something with sandpaper. You can run your fingers over the writing, and it's still rough. You sandpaper it until you don't feel the roughness. But it's not very conscious, and it certainly isn't theoretical in the slightest. Intuitive, I guess, is the word.

Interviewer: When did you decide that you had to be a writer?

Stegner: I'm a writer by the sheerest accident. Nobody in my family had ever gone to college, and at college they said,

"You've got to major in something," and so I said, "Fine. Economics," and I took one course in economics and that cured that. Then my freshman English teacher, who was Vardis Fisher, thought I had some kind of gift, so he let me out of two quarters of freshman English and put me in an advanced class, which gave me the notion that I could put words together . . . in some fashion. Then he went away, and I got another teacher who taught short story. I wrote some undergraduate short stories, won a little prize at one of the local newspapers. But I was selling rugs and linoleum for a living, and, as far as I knew, I would go on selling rugs and linoleum for a living. I'm writing this piece of stupidity into the novel I'm writing now [*Recapitulation*] because it seems to me nobody above the stage of a cretin could have been so completely unaware, so totally naive, so unsophisticated, wide-eye, going any way he was pushed. I was silly putty.

When I graduated from college finally, the head of the Psychology Department said, "Do you want to go on to graduate school?" I said, "Sure, where? How? In what?" He said, "I'll give you a fellowship in psychology." So I said, "Fine," and took it. When I went over to the English Department, the head of the English Department said, "You're out of your mind. You're not a psychologist. You're an English major! If you go to graduate school, you ought to go in English." I said, "But the man offered me a fellowship." "All right," he said, "We'll see if we can get you something." He got me a fellowship at the University of Iowa, so I dutifully trotted off to the University of Iowa to get an M.A. in English, and when I got there I found Norman Foerster, who had just come from the University of North Carolina or somewhere and was just founding the School of Letters, which became the whole mother of the Iowa Writing Program. Paul Engle and I were the first two, I suppose, who went through that shop. "Sure I like writing short stories, and I'd rather do that than learn *Beowulf*." I had to learn *Beowulf*, too, unhappily. But I took an M.A. in Creative Writing and wrote some stories and published one or two of them in a couple of little places.

I had a choice at that point about what I was going to do.
By then, the Depression was on. There wasn't anything to do.
If you were in college during the Depression, you were lucky,
because you didn't starve in college. There weren't many jobs
outside, so instead of going back to Salt Lake and selling rugs
and linoleum again—or whatever I was going to do—I just
stayed in college. I decided I couldn't get a job too readily with
a degree in writing, which, at that point, at least, was looked
down upon as a very low-life degree. So I took a Ph.D. in
American literature and went back to Salt Lake to teach, and
after two years of recovering from the Ph.D., I sat down one
afternoon and wrote a story just because I wanted to write a
story. I wrote it in about two hours and sent it off to somebody
—*Virginia Quarterly*, I think—and they published it. And, you
know, then you're hooked. By that time I was twenty-six or
twenty-seven, but I hadn't been grinding away at a literary
apprenticeship except for the M.A., and I had given writing
up as a possible career. It never occurred to me that there was
a possibility of making a living at it. So it was all pure, brute
accident, with some people who encouraged me along the
way. That's probably the way it is. You do get encouraged
when you're young and malleable by people who think they
know better than you do what you're good for. And they may
be right. Certainly I'd have made a terrible economist.

*Interviewer: You mention your degree in creative writing being looked
upon as a low-life degree. I think even today degrees in creative writing
are suspect in academic circles. Could you say something about that,
about the dichotomy that is said to exist between creative writing and
literature?*

Stegner: It seems to me—and I accept the exaggeration in what
I may be about to say—that many of the people teaching writing at the colleges that I know are actually teaching more about
love of literature, about how to read, even, than the people
who pretend to teach literature courses and put you through

all the marginalia of Gabriel Harvey and all the other clutter
that you get when you undertake a graduate degree. It used
to be literary history, and now it is literary criticism in the
English departments. Both of them seem to me moderately
pernicious.

Writing classes are something else. When you sit down to
write a story—whether under guidance or by yourself—you're
putting everything you know into that one little toothpaste
tube, and you're squeezing it out at the end. That's good. That's
synthetic in the best sense. It's not analytic. It's putting things
together rather than taking them apart. English departments
seem to take things apart, and they breed book-haters. I know
an awful lot of graduate students who read books in order to
despise them, in order to be able to put them down. To hell
with that. I don't really believe in that one bit.

*Interviewer: But you've edited and written
English department books, haven't you?*

Stegner: Not really, no. Two or three courses that I gave at
Stanford I put into books from the notes. One of them is in
a Rinehart Edition, *The Rise of Realism in American Literature.*
I've had a hand in a couple of writing texts, but they don't
really amount to much. I much prefer teaching writing
without a text. People ought to be reading all the time when
they're writing, or while they are learning to write, because
they are going to learn a lot of what they write from other
writers. That's the only place you can learn how language is
used plasticly to make new things. I don't think you can learn
it as rules or anything of the kind. Otherwise you come with
what I found a lot of Filipino writers doing.

In 1950 I went around the world for the Rockefeller Foundation, visiting writers in Asia and seeing what the world
looked like after the war. A whole bunch of Filipino writers
who were quite gifted were handicapped by the fact that the
only places they could publish were in the Sunday supplements

of the newspapers. But there they had a great market. All of them had published three hundred stories before they were twenty-five. They never got any better, and that was the trouble. They had no critical tradition. Nobody ever put them on the grindstone. These writers struck me by being very nimble in written English, but their spoken English was so very strange that I could barely understand them. They were eloquent on paper, but just incoherent, *viva voce*. It turned out that all of them had learned English surreptitiously from other Filipinos during the war. They had learned it under the gun, when it was a hanging offense or a shooting offense to teach English on the islands, so that after two or three removes from the real thing they were speaking Filipino English. It was a syllabic language, like Tagalog. It didn't run in phrases, as English ordinarily runs. So it was like East Indian English, and all but unintelligible to an American. I think you can't learn to write a language really well anymore than you can learn to speak a language really well without going to the people who speak and write it natively, and not only natively, but eloquently. If you are going to learn to write, then you had better go to the best writers, and the writers in your own tradition, whatever that may be. I don't think I would go to Jane Austen anymore. There are American writers whose idiom is closer to my own and who can teach me much more—more, for that matter, than Shakespeare.

Interviewer: What's the most difficult thing to teach about writing? And what's the most difficult thing for students to learn?

Stegner: That's a hard question. I can guess. Assuming that the student is at a stage where he is still teachable—there *is* a time when you shouldn't try to teach him, when he is as technically proficient and as subtle as you are or more so and has his own ways for going about what he wants to say, and what he wants to say may not be what you would say—one of the hardest things to teach him is *Revise! Revise! Revise!* And they won't revise, often. Many of them would rather write a new book than revise the old one. Revision is what separates the men from the boys. Sooner or later, you've got to learn to revise.

On the other hand, there's occasionally somebody like Bob Stone, who had the National Book Award, what, two years ago? (*Dog Soldiers*). Quite wacky, really. Quite mad. He got the notion in the middle of the year that he had a brain tumor. He came in and sat across from my desk and big drops of sweat formed on his forehead. "I'm going blind!" he said, scared to death. He had just used up his fellowship. So I quickly reinstated his fellowship so that he could get free medical care. He swore later they bored a hole into his head and blew him out with a pressure hose, but they didn't find any brain tumor. He came all bald-headed to a party when Bill Styron was there talking. He looked like Slick Watts or somebody. But he was one you couldn't teach *not* to revise. He was so finicky that it would take him a quarter to produce a chapter. He would be working on it all the time, but he wouldn't really let anybody see it until it satisfied him completely. He's an exception, though, and a very good writer.

Interviewer: If you were to outline a course of study for a writer at the outset of his undergraduate career, what would it include? Or is the question too broad?

Stegner: That's pretty broad. It might be different for every individual. I would ask some questions. I suppose I would say, "Are you a reader?" If you aren't a reader, you might as well forget trying to be a writer. I don't think that it's necessary to take a lot of courses in English literature. I sound prejudiced against the English departments, but in a sense, if you had some kind of guidance, if you had a tutor who could suggest books for you to read, it would be better, I think, than taking regular English department courses. And to know something substantive, to have some kind of skill, some body of knowledge, is terribly useful. I don't care what it is. It will be useful in writing sooner or later. If you only play tennis well, if you're a doctor—whatever you do. I know what I would do if I were doing it again. I would take courses in biology and anthropology, but that's my particular bias. Other people might think I ought to take psychology, which I don't trust as much as I do biology. Whatever your choice, there's no substitute for knowing something. As Benny DeVoto once said in a dour martini-lit moment, "Literary people always tend to overbid their knowledge." At the same time, while you're learning something, I suspect that you should keep writing. Use it or lose it. Creation is a knack which is improved by practice, and like almost any skill, it is lost if you don't practice it.

So you have to write and read, you should spend quite a lot of time learning some substantial body of knowledge, breaking your brain upon a problem which will let you incorporate in your own head much that is known about some little corner of the human tradition. With a whole university at your command, you can do it any way you want. You're very fortunate to have the university. A lot of people don't. Think of Tillie Olson.

I don't know whether you know Tillie Olson or not. She's only written five short stories in her life, but she's made those five stories carry her farther than a whole string of camels. She has ridden fifteen or twenty years on those five stories. Each one of them is a small gem, and her signature is so small you have to read it with a magnifying glass. Strange, intense, indrawn person. Well, she didn't have the university. She was the wife of a labor organizer in San Francisco in Harry Bridges's longshoreman's union. Eventually her husband quarreled with Harry, and Harry gooned him off the waterfront. He had to leave the labor movement and so he apprenticed himself to a printer. Tillie was feeding four or five daughters on an apprentice printer's wages, and for years she had no way of making contact with the literary world at all. She just had the San Francisco library, essentially, and she became what the IWWs used to call a "bughouse philosopher." A bughouse philosopher was somebody who spent a lot of time in the reading rooms of public libraries and had big ideas, often kind of askew because a homemade education doesn't have many corrections in it. Tillie had only that kind of education, but she had a great gift. She is a very powerful writer in the few things she has managed to complete. You're luckier than she is if you're one of those—like Henry James's boy—upon whom nothing is lost. If you're that kind, anything will stick to you. That particular knack of being human flypaper is one of the things that I kept looking for when we were picking fellows at Stanford. Another thing I kept looking for was seriousness of intention, seriousness of purpose, and willingness to sit down and really work at it without being driven to work at it. Any writer had better be a self-starting worker.

Another quality is the willingness to revise, to take criticism. And the fourth, which is often just whistling in the dark, is to know something. With those criteria, I think we managed to pick quite a few good writers at Stanford.

1 MARCH 1982
Los Altos Hills, California

Interviewer: I hope you don't mind me using a tape recorder.

Stegner: If you're gathering living history, I suppose they're essential, but for writing a book I would much rather make my notes just as I went.

Interviewer: Well, that's a subject I find interesting. Apparently, you and your character, Lyman Ward in Angle of Repose, *are at odds on this issue, because Lyman uses a tape recorder to write his book.*

Stegner: Yes, but any time you have somebody ostensibly speaking his own voice, you certainly—you have to—have Lyman's tone. You have to make the writing sound like a voice and not like some stultified preacher writing a sermon in a cold room. That's simply part of the whole package of verisimilitude, of plausibility. And it's particularly important, I think, when you're writing first-person narrative. The only other first-person narrative I've written (practically) are those other Joe—uh, what's his name?

Interviewer: Allston?

Stegner: Allston, and that's a different tone entirely. It's a much more flippant tone. It's not a scholarly tone, but it is still oral, I hope. And I hope it's a different tone than Lyman's, because if it isn't different, then people are reading me into both of those people, and I'm just making both of them mouthpieces.

Interviewer: Perhaps. But don't those people who confuse author with narrator have a legitimate viewpoint? In his introduction to Walden, *for example, Thoreau reminds us of something we commonly forget when we read: that it is* always *the first person who is speaking. Regardless, you would agree, wouldn't you, that readers want a sense of intimacy in a book?*

Stegner: I think there's a sense of intimate acquaintance that you look for in a book, yes. But I can get that out of a third-person narrator just as well as out of the first, I think.

Interviewer: But do you get the same *sense of intimacy from third-person narration as from first?*

Stegner: No, you don't. And one of the things that can happen when you're writing a first-person narrative is that you can insert some element of unreliability into the character without depreciating him. There's *Huckleberry Finn,* for instance, which is a beautiful example of first-person narrative. Huckleberry is not to be believed always. When he says, "All right, then, I'll go to hell," the reader understands exactly why he says that, but the reader is thinking the exact opposite. With a character like Lyman Ward, I have to have a reader believing in him pretty implicitly when he's talking about his grandmother. But when Lyman talks about himself, then the character isn't a whole.

I don't know if you can do the same thing in the third person, at least not without some labels and captions, which would make the narrative technique heavy-handed and pretty obvious. So that's one of the reasons why first person, for certain kinds of storytelling, seems to be better than third. For other kinds, when you don't have the problem of the reliability of the character, then it doesn't matter.

Interviewer: What is originality in fiction?

Stegner: I haven't the slightest idea. It's often thought to be technical innovation, experimentation of one kind or another, which never intrigued me, so I would deny that technical innovation or experimentation amounts to originality. But I don't know what originality is except, I suppose, that you can tell when it isn't there. If everything in your story can be anticipated from where you start, if you start with a situation, and the story develops in absolutely anticipated ways—to an anticipated conclusion—then I wouldn't say it's original. You're following a pattern which is practically imprinted on it. I suppose some element of the unexpected, or some element, at least, of the—what would you call it?—profound, I guess. To be original I would think you have to see so deeply into characters that you say something that makes a reader really pause, that isn't necessarily what he would have thought himself, at that point. And ultimately, you have to make him go your way, too.

Interviewer: For me, two of the most original novels to appear in the 1970's were John Fowles's The French Lieutenant's Woman *and your* Angle of Repose. *Both employ similar narrative techniques, some that we haven't seen in the novel for a long time. Is it possible that you could have read Fowles's novel either during or before the writing of* Angle of Repose?

Stegner: I read it with some concern, I confess, because I saw it when I was about two-thirds of the way through my book, when it was too late to change mine.

Interviewer: *Where did you read it?*

Stegner: Well, Fowles had just been here. You see, I know Fowles, and I read the book very early. I don't know whether I reviewed it or not, but I had an early copy. I know who did

review it: Ian Watt at Stanford. And then I guess I borrowed
his copy. Billy Abrahams and others were throwing some
parties for Fowles, and he was around here for several days.
Then I had him come to Clibdon—that was later, though
—to talk to the Stanford students there. He came down and
spent a night and a couple of days there. But that was long
after my qualms about, 'Do I have to rewrite this book just
because he got his out a few months before me?' That's the
way I remember it, anyway.

*Interviewer: Could we talk more about innovation and originality
in fiction? I look at both* Angle of Repose *and* The French
Lieutenant's Woman, *for example, and I see very traditional
novels, extremely traditional novels.*

Stegner: I think they are traditional, which doesn't bother me
one bit. I don't really aspire to write a novel which can be read
backwards as well as forward, which turns chronology on its
head and has no continuity and no narrative, which, in effect,
tries to create a novel by throwing all the pieces in the bag and
shaking the bag. It doesn't seem to me to be worth doing. So,
if you have to do *that* to be original, then I don't care about
being original. In fact, I don't think originality as it's usually
used is particularly useful. It's not a criterion that means much,
because it usually seizes upon some innovation that often turns
out to be frivolous or essentially unimportant, and which dis-
appears. An awful lot of mutations, which is what these things
are, turn out to be monsters. That can't live. I'm content with
the species, with turning out two-legged animals with one head.

*Interviewer: Speaking of monsters, could we talk about critics and
criticism a moment? Have you ever considered what happens when
a clever critic gets hold of a good novel? If he's clever enough—or
influential enough—he can fix the reading and interpretation of a
book that has so many other possibilities.*

Stegner: A critic can fix himself to a book like barnacles to a whale. Yes, that's true. I'm not sure he adds to the book, necessarily, but he can, as you say, impose himself on it, in a way. There is a sort of creativity that goes among critics.

Interviewer: Is there really? Tell me about it.

Stegner: They use a book as a basis for free association, for one thing.

Interviewer: Yes. Marvin Bell tells us in one of his poems how many times a critic reads a book: less than once. I suppose I'm simply bitter because I'm having a difficult time at the moment with a course in literary theory. It seems to me as if contemporary theorists of literature are unable to communicate even among themselves. I would prefer to make my living writing fiction and poetry and teaching them rather than criticism.

Stegner: Someone once remarked that the moment you begin to conceptualize you have lost touch with reality, and that literary theory is all about conceptualizing and literature ought to be about reality, somehow. Literature ought to be particular, not general. And you might be able to generalize from it, but it takes a secondary act to do that, and the thing itself ought to be just as alive as the tape. That's why I would have to agree with you, by and large, about a career in criticism. It doesn't seem to me to be more than a second-best choice. Maybe third. You've been teaching in the Writer's Workshop at Arizona?

Interviewer: No. I turned down the chance to do that because I love teaching literature. As an editor, I see enough contemporary writing. But I do want to continue teaching, if only so I'll have some time to write, more time than I would if I went back to construction or work in the woods.

Stegner: At least you get summers—and that matters. When you're as young as you are, you probably have the steam to go on writing even while you're teaching. I certainly did. But I got to an age where teaching got to be too much of a burden to carry, essentially two jobs. For a long time I carried two, and for a while three. That's a good way to get tired.

Interviewer: How do you feel about writing now that you've retired? I just finished reading a remarkable book—a first book—by a retired William Rainy Harper Professor from the University of Chicago.

Stegner: A River Runs Through It? Yeah, it's a good little book. A splendid book. I understand Norman Maclean is off in some cabin writing more, and I hope that's true. I was up in Idaho last week—

Interviewer: In Idaho?

Stegner: In Lewiston, yes. Lewis–Clark State College.

Interviewer: At Browning's place?

Stegner: You know Browning?

Interviewer: He's my publisher. One of them, anyway. What were you doing up there?

Stegner: I was lecturing, reading. I stayed with Browning. All the pheasants flew by his window. Beautiful. I had known Browning before, but Lewiston is a kind of interesting place, in its way, and one of the things that's clear is that Norman Maclean speaks like bugles for all those who live in that northwest country. A River Runs Through It is my kind of story. The people up there think highly of Maclean. I guess that's where I heard he was off writing more. I don't know how old Maclean is.

*Interviewer: Let's talk about the question of age and writing well.
I think Conrad started at age forty. Hardy, of course, wrote his best
poetry—*

Stegner: After Jude the Obscure.

*Interviewer: Yes, but contrary to popular
belief, writing well isn't a question of age.*

Stegner: I don't know anybody in this country who's writing
into a really advanced age and then writing pretty well. Except
Red Warren . . . who's . . . eighty?

Interviewer: Eighty-two, I believe.

Stegner: Malcolm Cowley wrote a book on being eighty,
but it's an old man's book. Malcolm is, I think, through
being a writer or a critic. His energy is kind of run down.
But Warren's doesn't seem to. So there. You're right. There
are a few. Sophocles wrote *Oedipus of Polonus* when he was
ninety. Goethe wrote a few things when he was very old. But
those are people with remarkable vigor, which lasts some way.
Not just anybody can do it. Some people are senile at sixty,
some at twenty.

Interviewer: What about Wallace Stegner? Can he do it?

Stegner: I don't know. I started another novel a while back. I
may not finish it, but I'll finish it if I can.

Interviewer: Can you talk about it?

Stegner: Well, the writing goes a lot slower than it used to.
But no, I don't think I can talk about the novel because it's
only on about page forty or so. But it does go very, very
slowly. I've been two months writing forty pages.

Interviewer: That doesn't sound so bad to me.

Stegner: When I was in my prime, so to speak, I would generally get anywhere from three to five or six pages a day, stuff that might have to be rewritten tomorrow, but which would essentially stay. That doesn't happen. It takes lots of combing to do it now.

Interviewer: Maybe you're just a harsher critic than you used to be. You once told me something about writing books that proved useful, even though you said it incidentally. You told me that the critic inside the writer ought to come to the work at a "different" hour than the writer. We were talking about revision.

Stegner: Well, I still think that's true. It's important to *get on* with the writing, particularly when you're young and you can hardly wait to get down to work because you're boiling with something. But I'm not boiling with anything anymore, and the critic is taking charge and I'm just driving the cab. So that's why it takes me so much longer, now, I'm sure.

Interviewer: Lyman Ward, your narrator in Angle of Repose*, is a pretty good critic, I'd say. Maybe you ought to resurrect him.*

Stegner: Well, Lyman is not a literary critic. He's a historian. That is to say, a person accustomed to looking fairly calmly at human behavior.

Interviewer: If Lyman's isn't a literary critic, then why is he doing an edition of The Scarlet Letter*?*

Stegner: You want the real answer?

Interviewer: Yeah. That would be helpful.

Stegner: Because Molly Foote did. She was an illustrator and she was doing the illustrations for a nineteenth-century gift book edition.

Interviewer: Yes. But the historical personage, Mary Hallock Foote, and your fictional creation of her as Susan Burling Ward—those are two different people. Molly Foote also did the illustrations for Longfellow, the New England poet.

Stegner: Yes. I guess some of the things you mention I invented and some of them I simply took off her track record. But if I had had her doing something else, *Leaves of Grass*, it wouldn't have been right. I would have falsified.

Interviewer: Yes, but you had the alternative. Lyman could have chosen to edit something else. But he chooses The Scarlet Letter *to talk about, and there seem to be some definite resemblances between* The Scarlet Letter *and* Angle of Repose. *I'd guess Hester Prynne was lurking somewhere in your soul or your psyche when you were conjuring up your own characters.*

Stegner: Hester lurks in all our souls, I think. It's possible. But remember. Molly Foote was doing other things, too. She did the *Skeleton in the Armory*. Do you think there is a skeleton lurking in your closet, maybe?

Interviewer: Well, maybe I am reading things into the novel that aren't there. But the literary allusions in Angle of Repose *seem to me to echo much of the entire canon of American literature from Hawthorne through Melville and James. For example, Lyman meets an old school chum on the street. This guy's a curiosity in many ways. Right?*

Stegner: A freak, yes.

Interviewer: Essentially, he's Argus-eyed. He's a washing machine repairman, and to repair the machines he has to wear lenses that magnify his vision. The guy also has a terrible speech impediment.

Lyman pities him but says something close to what Ishmael tells us in
Moby Dick*: "Who ain't a slave?"*

Stegner: I wasn't remembering that. I think the final line of that
chapter is, "Whose head isn't inside a Bendix?"

Interviewer: Yeah.

Stegner: But I was talking about vision, tunnel vision, space
being curved. You wind up looking at the back of your own
neck. Those are the kinds of thoughts Lyman gets from living
in a wheelchair, I suppose, because he can't bend his neck. At
the same time, I did draw from all sorts of elements of reality. I
knew a guy with a wart on his tongue, and I never did understand why some kind soul didn't help him go to a doctor and
get it off. With that speech—and all the kids he taught being
unable to understand him—poor booger—he went through
life with a curse. But I also knew a fella who fixed Bendix
washing machines who had quadrafocals, too, and he really
did look like a fly's eye. So I put them together, and they did
seem to have something to do with the problem of vision as
it bothers a man like Lyman, going into town and hating it,
running into social contacts which are uncomfortable for him.
A thing like that you don't think out until you put it down as
it might happen on the street. And that sort of scene writes
itself very fast. That whole chapter, I'm sure, I did in a morning and never revised. But other parts I had to comb over,
preen and file and sandpaper.

*Interviewer: Okay. But hold on a minute here. As a young man
you wrote a piece for* Saturday Review, *I believe, called "Fiction:
A Lense on Life." Put that together with James's "House of Fiction"
introduction to* The Portrait of a Lady *and all that goes on in* Angle
of Repose. *What's a poor graduate student to do?*

Stegner: No. I don't think that's true. Some of those allusions I intended, some of them may have been unconscious—because one has read James a lot. But some of them may be pure accident, too. There are three possibilities, at least. About the ones that are unconscious: I'm sure writers make a lot of those if they have the same kind of memory I do in which words stick. Other things don't stick. But words do. That kind of thing, whether it's unconscious or not, is a legitimate critical point. It's just lucky or unlucky. It can go either way.

Interviewer: All right. Let's talk about your character from All the Little Live Things, *Jim Peck, and that original Peck's bad boy from American literature, Henry Thoreau. Where does Peck live around here, anyway?*

Stegner: He lives down in those big trees down there, down on the bottom, down there across the creek. Actually there was a fellow who lived down there, not in a tree, but in a tent for a year or two, and he lived across the creek among the poison oak so as to make himself as remote as possible. But that's commonplace. Now the house is owned by some people named Prudence, who sold that bottomland several years ago. So you can't go there anymore. You can't make any literary excursions to that shrine. You couldn't see anything anyway. Just poison oak and a big old bay tree.

Interviewer: Well, Peck would seem to represent the "native" element in American literature. Would you agree?

Stegner: Well, there are three pretty good writers I know of to do that. Scott Momaday is probably the most visible Indian writer you can name, without going to Poland. I don't know Cheyenne [Hyemeyohsts] Storm, but I have read Leslie Silko, who's a good writer. You could put together a pretty good anthology out of just those three or four people.

Interviewer: Let's get back to another subject. I'm thinking of All the

Little Live Things, Angle of Repose, *and* The Spectator Bird. *It seems that you've had more success—commercial success—with first-person fiction than with third.*

Stegner: I don't know that it's markedly true. Actually, *Big Rock Candy Mountain* was, to some extent, a commercial success, and that's not first-person. I suppose the book that has sold the most around the world and has been translated into more languages is one I shrink at a little, and that's *A Shooting Star.* Which is likewise not first-person.

Interviewer: Perhaps I'm only thinking of recent novels, like Recapitulation.

Stegner: Is Recapitulation first-person?

Interviewer: Seems like the cutting you read at Arizona was.

Stegner: I've forgotten. In fact, I'd written it three ways. I wrote it in the first person, and I wrote it in the third. And I think it wound up in the third. It began as a first-person narrative by somebody quite different from Bruce Mason. Then, because I saw a chance to cannibalize a couple of short stories that were spin-offs from *The Big Rock Candy Mountain,* and because I really wanted to write a book about my love for Salt Lake in the twenties, I thought: all right, exactly. That fits the tail end of *The Big Rock Candy Mountain,* so why don't I switch it over and make it the survivor of the *Big Rock Candy Mountain.* But it wound up in third person.

Interviewer: Would you accept the notion that your first-person novels have been more highly regarded?

Stegner: I think most people consider *Angle of Repose* the best book. *Spectator Bird* also got an award, and both of those are first-person, so that adds a certain weight to your theory. . . .

One critic of my work, Forrest Robinson, would probably beat around this notion that I have been somewhat like Conrad and found my voice when I discovered somebody to speak through, like Marlow. I'm not sure that's right.

Interviewer: But it is a problem, especially now in the wake of the modest body of Stegner criticism that has begun to appear. Much of it confuses Wallace Stegner with the narrators of his novels like Joe Allston and Lyman Ward. Can we talk about how you choose the names of your characters?

Stegner: Sure. Which ones?

Interviewer: How about Lyman Ward? I know his etymology. There are both Wards and Lymans in the actual family tree of the family whose history you borrow for Angle of Repose. *But Lie-Man —what a wonderful name for a storyteller. And* Ward: *aren't we back to Ishmael and the American Orphan? Accident or design?*

Stegner: Pure accident. I think I probably named him Lyman because the president of Stanford at that time was named Dick Lyman, and I just borrowed his name. Ward, I don't know where I picked up Ward except for Judy Ward Howe and so on. I wanted an old, eastern, established name. Even though Ward came a little close to some of the ancestors of the people I used as models, I still felt it was legitimate. It wasn't the name of either family. It was on a collateral edge of one of the families. So that's where it came from, I suppose. I also wanted to use the fella in Leadville, the wizard of Wall Street, the man who broke Ulysses Grant and more or less disgraced him.

Interviewer: Who was that?

Stegner: Sam Ward. He was a speculator who got next to Grant. He appears in the book just briefly as a kind of foil for the relatively square, unimaginative integrity of his cousins.

Interviewer: How long did Angle of Repose *take to write?*

Stegner: About three years, I guess. But it's hard to say how long a big book like that takes, because I was teaching pretty well to the end of it. I finished it while I was at the English campus of Stanford. I took it to Doubleday's office in London. So I know *when* I finished it. I finished it in the summer of 1970. But I'd been working on it at least three years before that and teaching some. My general schedule was to teach a full load of courses in two quarters in order to get two quarters off in consecutive order. So, I'd write six months, and then I'd pretty well be off six months, and I'd come back on it for six months. So when I say it took me three years, it took me essentially half of that.

Interviewer: Wasn't Rodman Paul, the editor of Molly Foote's own autobiography, working on his edition at the same time you were turning Foote into the character of Susan Burling Ward?

Stegner: Rodman Paul is the grandnephew of Mary Hallock Foote. He was mad at me, as a matter of fact. Not all the family were. But he got upset at something. Between us, we've more or less revived Molly Foote, though. She was dead as a doornail before we began working on those papers.

Interviewer: But Paul was editing the autobiography, right?

Stegner: Yes, but there were two manuscripts. One, I think, is at the Huntington Library now, and one is at Stanford. I'm not sure which is earlier. I think the longer one, which he used. Mary Foote tried, when she was unable to sell the longer one, to cut it down to make it more palatable to the publisher. And that's probably the one we have at Stanford. It could be checked out. I can get the papers down here.

Interviewer: Did you know he was working on the papers?

Stegner: I didn't know he was working on the papers, but I did know he was related to her.

Interviewer: So you didn't *know he was working on the autobiography?*

Stegner: Not when I . . . see, I published the book, I finished writing the book in the summer of 1970, and his was copyrighted in 1972. I don't know how long he worked on it, but essentially I quit working on the papers in 1968 or 1969. I copied them all and took them to Vermont and spent one whole summer doing nothing but reading those damn letters over and over, just to see what kind of book was in them. I knew there was a book there, but I wasn't quite sure what it was. I had thought of writing her biography, as apparently he was doing. I decided, quite frankly, that she wasn't worth a biography. She wasn't an important enough literary person, though she was pretty good. And her art was hard to judge, because she drew so commonly, particularly in later life, directly onto wood blocks, so that there are no originals. Everything is a copy, a printed version of the original. The originals are copper plates or wood blocks, and some of those, I think are at the Huntington. But all I've ever seen of her art is in publications like *Century* and *Scribners*. So I decided against writing a biography. I wanted her to cast a bigger shadow than that interesting but rather modest success that she had had as a Victorian gentlewoman with gifts. So I began to think *novel*. And it took quite a lot of reading through the papers and absorbing them and finding out where they said something between the lines. And where I deliberately wanted to change, where I decided I really didn't want to follow the life, then I changed. It's always more fun when you can make up the life. I borrowed an awful lot from hers. The whole structure of the novel can be found in her papers. Except the Lyman Ward part, which is all invention. I really didn't want to write a simple, one-track triangle story, either, or a story about the winning of the West. I wanted history to reverberate with the present. So that's why Lyman Ward got invented: so that he and his grandmother could play back and forth.

Interviewer: Oh, yes. Hawthorne's problem again: lack of a usable past. That's still a real problem for most writers in the contemporary West.

Stegner: Particularly to the West, because we've given our heart to the foolish Old West myth so wholly, so much so that we think of *that* as our history, which it isn't.

Interviewer: Not at all?

Stegner: I never knew any . . . yes, I did. I knew one gunfighter. He was killed by a Mountie in the streets of Shonovan up in Saskatchewan. And he really wasn't a gunfighter, he was just a Montana cowpuncher who got a little drunk and carried a gun against regulations, and the Mountie shot him.

Interviewer: Let's come back to this subject. You've written several kinds of books: straight fiction, fictional biography, and biography. Isn't a biography really fiction?

Stegner: There's certainly a large component of invention that goes into any biography: if nothing else, selection, because simply by selection you begin to change the reality. Malcom Cowley wrote me a note. He didn't like Bernard DeVoto very well, but he liked the biography. He said, "What you've written is a novel." I guess it probably is, although I was staying with the facts, so far as I could find them out. And I didn't even speculate very much about motivation and so on, unless I knew from letters or from talking to Benny—or having talked to him or his wife or some other source—about what he was feeling at a particular time. I wouldn't say there's any invention of fact in *The Uneasy Chair*, but there's certainly some invention in what you might call the storyline. It's all suggested in the life, and it's all essentially there, but you can certainly firm that line up and maybe make that book from DeVoto's rebellion against Ogden, Utah, and his going East to make his fortune in the land of brains and intelligence.

Interviewer: But whether writing fictional biography or straight biography, a writer has to accept certain "givens," doesn't he?

Stegner: Mary Hallock Foote didn't die until she was ninety-two. And I wasn't going to follow her life that long. That's one of the reasons I had to give her a catastrophe. Her daughter didn't drown in a ditch at all at the age of five or six. She died of a ruptured appendix at seventeen. So there was that tragedy in her life. This was a favorite daughter and so on. But I just moved it back and drowned the poor child like a kitten a little younger. That's all right, I think. I wasn't writing biography, I was writing a novel. Then I told her granddaughter, who had given me the papers, I wanted to write a novel, and she said, "Fine, sure, do what you want." But then that made a problem for my acknowledgment, because I couldn't say, "Thanks to the Foote family for the use of this material," because that would have led all kinds of people to believe that the book was frankly autobiographical, which some still believe anyway. For the same reason, they believe every narrator I invent is me. They can't read books any other way, I think.

Interviewer: Isn't the process of writing itself a theme in your fiction?

Stegner: Angle of Repose, a good part of it, the whole Lyman Ward part, is about process, the process that a Ph.D. candidate would go through digging out the stuff for his dissertation. It's essentially literary detective work, library research, it's called "survey." That process is there, and I used it, quite frankly, as the framework for that whole element of the story. *The Uneasy Chair* was a pretty straightforward kind of biographical investigation, complicated by the fact that I had known Benny

DeVoto very well. It's always more difficult to write about somebody you know well. For one thing, it presents you with the problems of how much to tell: things that are nobody's damn business, and you don't want to embarrass your friends or your friend's wife or your friend's family with something that has nothing to do with the main subject you're writing about. In my case, it was Benny's career, the way his head worked, and what he did with his head. He was a kind of neurotic, and he did some kind of silly things in his life, but it didn't seem to me it was essential to spell out all the silly things. So in a sense I suppose I can be called a whitewasher.

Interviewer: You mean that what you've written of DeVoto is not the life of Bernard DeVoto but rather a life. I could come along and do some detective work and write another life, right?

Stegner: Sure.

Interviewer: There was a problem in writing about DeVoto because you were so close, then?

Stegner: And I didn't want to leave out his warts, because he was all warts. And you have to be honest without being unkind, I think, honest without being a muckraker. There isn't an awful lot of muck in his life to rake, but wherever there was, I didn't even want to know about it, especially. He was susceptible to infatuations with young women, which never came to anything, but it made him look silly. He kind of had that Hand Maiden myth in his mind, and some violet-eyed dowry was always leading him by the hand and bathing his brow in his imagination. Which you could make a lot of, if you wanted to, or nothing. Maybe I made a little bit of it. A lot of the Kate Stern thing, if you remember, was like that. A tubercular girl, she was made to order for Benny, because she appealed to every sentimental cell in him. Nice girl, doomed, it was a touching situation. He wrote that girl two or three letters a week for ten or twelve years, and he took down his hair with her much more than he did with most of his close friends. A lot of the way I know some intimate things about him came to me from those letters, which are sealed now. They're nobody's business. We thought there might be a book in those letters, because it is sort of a touching situation. Never met her. But I think it would not be a good thing to publish.

Interviewer: Why?

Stegner: Simply because he couldn't help being fatuous, given the situation. Seeing himself in sort of self-congratulatory postures, looking after this poor girl and being fatherly—he fancied the fatherly pose—instructing her in all the arts of life and imagination and being kindly and benevolent and the rest. She adored him, obviously, but he was a little fatuous. She wouldn't have noticed it, but an outsider does.

Interviewer: Or an insider. But how do you know when you look at the leavings from a life whether to write the novel or the biography? Couldn't we say the same thing of DeVoto that you said of Mary Foote? Is he really important enough for a biography? I mean, it's true that DeVoto wrote novels, but when we read them now . . .

Stegner: No. DeVoto really was a voice. He was not only a representative and vocal westerner, who spoke from a western point of view in places where that was not particularly popular or understood, but who also, as in the land-grab situation in forty-seven, did a vast public service and who, as the editor or the writer of *"The Uneasy Chair"* for a little more than twenty years, was a voice that people harkened to and listened to and went to *Harper's* to read every month. I think he probably spoke more people's minds than Molly Foote did, and while you can't make him significant in the way Franklin Delano Roosevelt was, one could choose to do that kind of a biography. I think DeVoto's biography is legitimate in many ways, because he does throw a shadow longer than himself. That would be my test on Molly Foote, too. I wanted her to throw a shadow longer than herself. If I'd have left her biographical, she wouldn't have.

Interviewer: But couldn't you have done the same thing with DeVoto?

Stegner: A novel about him? I suppose I could.

Interviewer: I wonder, for example, if it isn't really the writing that casts the shadow you're talking about rather than the life.

Stegner: I don't know. I got an awful lot of grateful letters on that biography of Benny. All kinds of people who had lived by his word were grateful to have him nailed up there on a pedestal of sorts, and just yesterday, as a matter of fact, somebody sent me a manuscript whose burden, in effect, was, "Where are you now, DeVoto, now that we need you?" And I think DeVoto was a public force. He knew a lot of quite important men and influenced them. He influenced Adlai Stevenson, for instance, and if Stevenson had happened to become president, DeVoto would have been—

Interviewer: I would have voted for him.

Stegner: Yes, so would . . . but you didn't have a chance to!

Interviewer: No. But I remember my parents. Stevenson was the man.

Stegner: Well, we missed it.

Interviewer: How much contemporary writing do you read now?

Stegner: I find myself, in the last fifteen or twenty years, getting

more and more to the position where I read only what I have
to read in order to write what I have to write if I'm doing any
journalism or historical jobs or anything like that. And then I'll
get a spell, as you do. Somebody will put me on a judging
board for the Pulitzer Prize or the Book Award or something,
and I'll have to read 200 novels in six months. And that gets to
be bedlam. I don't see very many novels that I want to read in
the current marketplace. I want to read Saul Bellow's. I understand it's dull, but he's never unintelligent. He may be a little
short on movement. Johnny Cheever has a new one, a little
one. I don't know what else I would feel I have to read. Maybe
Tom McGuane, who used to be a student here, though I
haven't found myself enchanted with the last couple. Too clever.

*Interviewer: Speaking of cleverness and Tom McGuane, have you
seen the recent piece in the* New York Times *entitled "New Writers
of the Purple Sage"? It lists you as Bill Stegner, Dean of Western
American Writers. Photo of McGuane in a big cowboy hat against
the backdrop of the Montana skyline.*

Stegner: Well, the caption was not very flattering. But the
selection of people, many of whom had been Stegner fellows,
I had to feel good about. Momaday's an Indian, all right, but a
good writer, too. Ed Abbey is somebody that you've got to pay
attention to. But the essential problem, as you say, is still with
us. And the editor who got that picture of McGuane or probably posed the picture himself is perpetuating precisely the
kind of thing that makes western writing second-rate. I think
the guy who wrote the piece had never read anything of mine
except probably that essay called "Born a Square," which ends,
I think, with a kind of prediction that sooner or later somebody
will have to do for the West what Faulkner did for the South
before the West will ever be accepted as a place where you can
write books. I wasn't so terribly pleased with being "the Dean
of Western Writers."

Interviewer: On that note, I think I'll leave so you can go to your reception for Ansel Adams.

Stegner: I'm sorry I can't offer you something to eat. My chores after five are to go by the grocery store. As you can see, one of the things we don't live next door to is the corner drug or the corner grocery store. So that every time you do go to get something, you have to go when you're absolutely out. I hate to waste the gasoline.

Interviewer: Good for you.

3 JANUARY 1987
Los Altos Hills, California

Interviewer: As a writer, do you consciously go in search of book projects? How did your new novel, Crossing to Safety, *begin? What triggered your responses?*

Stegner: No. I don't go in search of projects. Sometimes they appear before my eyes, and sometimes they grow over a long period of time as I brood about something. Sometimes I know there's a book there, and I have to hunt through an awful lot of research materials, as I did with *Angle of Repose*, which we've spoken of before. That was a very gradual process. I have started books without knowing where they were going to end, too. That's more dangerous. But in the case of *Crossing to Safety*, the book just grew, more or less, through a lot of personal experience in Vermont, and, to a smaller extent, in Wisconsin, and to a small extent, in Italy. Those places seemed to me places where what was gradually developing in my mind could find a home. That's how the book came about. And it took a long time. I had to do it by trial and error, and I was years getting it finally sorted out. It's not a conscious process.

Interviewer: Was there any point where you definitely knew this project was a novel?

Stegner: I knew from the beginning it was going to be a book. You have that feeling. It's like having a fish on. You know when it's an old boot and when it's a fish. But I didn't know | 77 what the book was. I've got piles of manuscript over there, eight and ten inches high, of stuff that's been written and tossed aside in the process of finding out. At several points the novel was going in entirely different directions. It had different characters from those that now appear, more characters, episodes that never got into the book at all. It started in a different place. It proceeded toward a different ending. As it worked out, the book compacted itself into a single day, and in the course of that single day, it gave me the opportunity to recapitulate four lives—the companionship, at least, of those two couples, the Morgans and the Langs. In the beginning, when I began the novel, both of the well-to-do couple, the Langs, were dead. I had the Morgans going back to the funeral of the second one. It finally wound up that the Morgans go back for the death of the first one, and we have the second one more or less in limbo. I ended by concentrating on one critical day.

Interviewer: Do you know in your own mind, then, all of the raw material from which this novel is made?

Stegner: Some of the novel, of course, is close to personal experience. The experience of the Morgans, the New Mexico couple, the unadvantaged pair, draws to some extent upon my experience and my wife's, although she never contracted polio and is not crippled for life. Many of the disasters that I visited upon her never happened to her but have happened to people we knew. I've known enough people with polio to know how often the disease seems to enlarge the humanity of the people who have it. It not only gives them health of a fragile kind until they collapse entirely, but it also does something to their souls, I think. I did want to write up particularly one woman whom we knew. She became close to saintly as a result of having had polio. That isn't personal experience exactly, but I've witnessed it. Other things in the book—Madison, Wisconsin, in the Depression; sharing an office with William Ellery Leonard; the business of the over-achiever—that is all out of my own

experience. I taught at Wisconsin for two years, and I stole a
few details for the novel. I could have put that whole thing at
a university like Michigan or Minnesota or Ohio State, some
midwestern school that I didn't know as well. But I saw no
reason to do so, since Wisconsin did leave a lot of echoes in
my head.

Interviewer: Why set so much of the novel in Vermont?

Stegner: Why not? I set it there because Vermont is a place I
know, and I like to write about places I know. Moreover, there
was a Thoreauvian impulse in Sid Lang, one of my characters
in this book, and Vermont is a good place to play Thoreau. It
would have been a different book and the impulse would have
been different if I hadn't laid it in New England, I think, because
Sid's background—though he comes from Pittsburgh—is essentially shaped by a New England conscience, a New England
cultural conscience, that personal culture Emerson and
Thoreau talked about, the business of constantly trying to make
yourself the best you can be. That's not western in any sense.
It's actually Transcendentalist, I suppose. So I used Vermont
for a number of reasons: (1) I knew it, and (2) it seemed to
match the characters I was shaping.

*Interviewer: Is the new novel in any way
a departure from your earlier fiction?*

Stegner: You seem to have it in mind that I generally write
about the West, which is true enough. But I would hate to
be imprisoned in it.

*Interviewer: No. I have it in mind that you are
an American writer, maybe even a world writer.*

Stegner: Yes. I do know some parts of the world. I laid half
of *The Spectator Bird* in Denmark, half of it right here. Other

books I have set in other parts of the country, and books like *Angle of Repose* and *Big Rock Candy Mountain* have covered quite a lot of ground. In this case, I was once again simply creating what seemed to me a fitting background for the story and the people that were taking shape in my head, relying, as it seems I must, on personal experience to some extent.

Interviewer: In writing Crossing to Safety, *did you confront any technical challenges you had never faced before?*

Stegner: There were problems in this book, partly because it's a very quiet book. Not much happens in it. It contains none of the things that seem to be essential for contemporary novels.

Interviewer: Well, it's not sensational . . .

Stegner: And not very active. Much of what goes on goes on in the mind, in memory. I was doing something that I would have advised almost any student of mine not to do: I let nearly the whole book happen in one head, during the course of one day. There's a little bit of front-stage action during the day, but most of the book curls back and picks up the past. That's a problem. It's a problem to do it without being dull. It's a problem to do it without being slow and tedious. I don't know if I succeeded or not. But I had to work on that problem constantly to keep the storyline from appearing to sag and go nowhere. It had to have some forward motion. It had to have some draft. That's a technical problem: by the pure force of the writing to create a sense of involvement in real events. Also the problem of how to get into the space of one day the essence of four lives is not small. I had done something like that before but never in such a concentrated way.

Interviewer: Yes, in Recapitulation. *But aren't these two dramatically different novels, thematically as well as technically?*

Stegner: Well, Larry Morgan is another person entirely from Bruce Mason. Bruce Mason is remembering the kind of bruising childhood that leaves him spiritually limping in *Recapitulation*: the dominant father and all the unhappy childhood, which really comes out of *The Big Rock Candy Mountain*. That experience is very different from the experience of somebody like Larry Morgan who grows up in a lower middle-class household as the son of an Albuquerque, New Mexico, mechanic, as a child whose family have always been helpful, friendly, supportive, but are now simply wiped out. Larry is an orphan, as Bruce Mason is, but an orphan without so many traumata, without, I think, the spiritual injuries that the ambassador in *Recapitulation* has. It's a different mind. In making fiction, one of the things a writer must do is to make absolutely certain that he knows the mind he's dealing *through*. In *Recapitulation,* I was dealing in third person, but through a particular memory and a particular mind. Here I'm dealing in first person, and I have to try to become that person as far as possible. If I succeed, I get the tone of voice and the quality of mind that will persuade a reader to see and hear a real and credible human being, not a mouthpiece or a construct. If fiction is going to be successful, Henry James said, it depends helplessly upon that sense of reality.

Interviewer: Verisimilitude. You have to convince the reader that the world the reader is entering is the real world and not the world of dream or memory only. Is that it?

Stegner: I believe the real world exists. I haven't any philosophical doubts about that. Moreover, before you can convince the reader, you have to convince yourself that, in effect, you have invaded and become the person you're speaking through. Every morning you have to read over what you did yesterday, and if it doesn't persuade you, it has to be redone. Sometimes it takes me three hours in the morning to get over the feeling that I've been wasting my time for the past week and that everything I've written up to that point is drivel. Until I can convince myself that I am speaking in the plausible, believable voice of the person I have invented, I can't go on. So the first job is to convince yourself, the second is to convince the reader. If you do the first, the second more or less follows.

Interviewer: In Crossing to Safety, *you seem to have created fiction from what, in earlier books, you often threw away. I'm thinking, for instance, of Sid and Charity Lang, two characters that seem marvelously free to make unimpeded moral choices that sometimes form crucial moments in the novel. While they have familial responsibilities, neither has any money problems. Like certain James characters, Sid and Charity can afford to move at will through the world you have created for them. I don't know if there's a question here, but I'd like a response.*

Stegner: No. You're absolutely right. I was deliberately making Sid and Charity people with all the advantages and all the freedoms of Henry James characters, not to emphasize a moral choice, as James often does, but to illustrate how, with everything going for them, these two people could get in each other's road. Their relationship, the thing that means the most to each of them, is actually an impediment to them both. That difficulty has something to do with the original title of the manuscript I sent you, *Amicitia*, with friendship; it has something to do with what personal relations do to people who would otherwise seem completely untrammeled. This girl, Charity, for instance, is a most generous, outgoing, willing, and helpful kind of person. She wants to do well. She wants to do good. She is implacably generous, implacably goodwilled, and it's the implacability of her goodness that ultimately brings down the house. You can call it a fault. You can call it a tragic flaw. You can call it whatever you want. It's part of her nature, which she is never going to get over and cannot possibly control. She is born to rule the roost. Even when she's doing the friendliest, most generous things, she's going to do them her way. She can't help doing them that way, and her goodwill can be disastrous. It's a rueful kind of message to make a novel out of.

Interviewer: You're also flip-flopping traditional roles the culture advocates for each of the sexes, aren't you?

Stegner: I think a lot of New England women are a little bit like Charity. Not, perhaps, in that extreme shape, but there have been many very able and rather dominant women in New England history, possibly because, as I suggested in the book, so many New England men went first to the gold rush, then to the Civil War, and never came back. A lot of women were left alone in New England towns. I don't know whether you know the stories of Mary Wilkins Freeman and people like that. Stories like "A New England Nun," about the old-maid-ism in New England, about women left behind by men who went elsewhere—to sea—went wherever they went. It's a common New England story from mid-nineteenth century up to well past the Civil War. These women had their own culture and cultivation, but the men who remained or came in were likely to be people of another culture—or of a lower social class. There was simply, for many superior women, no adequate supply of men. Necessity bred a certain amount of self-sufficiency among New England women; I've known a lot of them. Charity I made into quite an extreme case, because I was trying to say something about the rueful underside of friendship, affection, love. Some people who have read the manuscript think of Charity as a monster. I didn't and don't think of her as a monster at all. I think of her as a prisoner of her own nature.

Interviewer: Can we properly speak of traditional forms in fiction in the same sense that we can speak of traditional forms in poetry? Probably not. But how can we or should we think of form in terms of fiction?

Stegner: Sonnets and rondels, no. But it seems to me every story has its own form, which can't be imposed upon the material but must be discovered within it. I don't believe, for instance, in such a thing as an all-inclusive form at all, because I don't think there is such a thing in philosophy, either. I don't believe in method makers, system makers; it doesn't seem to me that life conforms to systems. Only systems conform to systems. The people who feel compelled to make systems, whether out of philosophy or out of human life, or out of words, are deluding themselves. I would rather follow the flow of life as it happens rather than of life as I can imagine it to be.

I don't think straitjackets are the way to get at fiction. I would rather define the novel as Stendahl did, as a mirror in the roadway. That goes far enough for me. Whatever happens in the road is going to happen in the mirror, too. You can't systematize that.

Interviewer: Then what about genres? Or what about the form of allegory you apparently employ against itself in the new novel: the man in the roadway with the mangled hand, the two Christs? You recall the section of the new book I'm referring to, don't you?

Stegner: Well, there are two Gardens of Eden, too. Allegory, hardly. That's just a glancing metaphor I'm employing there. I certainly don't intend any kind of Faerie Queen kind of allegory. It does seem to me that when people find themselves in a beautiful natural setting like the one in the novel, and things are going well, and they love what they are doing and the people they are with, then inevitably some kind of garden myth arises in their heads. *This is paradise, this is the best it's ever been.* It's hard to speak of such experiences in any other terms than the paradisiac terms of the garden. But I certainly didn't—

Let's start over. There *is* a snake in there. I mention a snake. But again, it's not an allegory. All allegory is a system. This is a metaphor.

Interviewer: Maybe. What about the working man with the mangled hand who at once embodies the spirit of the place and possesses the very eyes of those we see in the two Pierro de la Francesca paintings of Christ?

Stegner: I may have a hard time convincing you of this, but those elements worked their way into the novel, not because I wanted an allegory in there. Those experiences happened. Gubbio, Italy, when we visited, was an untouched, virtually medieval town, beautiful, the same town where Zefferelli filmed *Romeo and Juliet.* The scenes in question are actually a close representation of personal experience, including the guy with the mangled hand. We were driving through the Apenines and came upon an accident where there had been a rock slide. We took the injured man to his village—he wouldn't let us take him to a doctor. He just put his hand up against his chest and marched up the hill. We were left confused, wondering what we should have done and could have done, and nothing we could conceive of could we have done because he wouldn't have let us. And also, if you know Pierro de la Francesca's painting, you know why I gave the injured workman those eyes. It's not invented purposefully. It is seized upon. The other day I quoted you Picasso—"I don't seek, I find." Well, here's something I found. It was there in my experience and my memory and it suited the circumstance, and I could make something of it.

But the direction from which the writing is approached does make a difference. I don't think of myself as an allegorist at all, and I shudder when you suggest I am. Any writer has to be able to perceive meaning in what he is writing, to select from what he knows in order to illuminate meaning, but the self-conscious Hawthornian kind of allegory is something that has never appealed to me. It seems to me meaning ought to arise spontaneously, just as things cast a shadow in the sun. To impose meaning is a falsification, even when you're as good as Hawthorne.

Interviewer: Still, judging by the whole body of your fiction, you seem to me a highly self-conscious novelist. I mean that as a compliment, although I don't think you're going to take it as one.

Stegner: That depends on what you mean by "self-conscious." I think I'm not careless, and I don't like to write things that fail to cast any shadow at all. On the other hand, I do, as I said, like to follow the flow of what I perceive to be the reality of ob-served life. I don't like to risk messing with that. If I'm lucky, things will come together. Let me give you now a little extra.

That Italian section was the last piece of the novel, practically, that I wrote. I inserted it. I simply stuck it in because it seemed to me there was a part of their lives undealt with, a gap there that needed to be closed. And I have lived in Italy, and I have had some of this experience. Italy seemed to me a place where I could play variations on the theme of companionship—again isolated, almost as in the Vermont woods, because the Morgans and the Langs are strangers in a foreign country. In Italy, also, I could emancipate this unlucky boy from New Mexico and his crippled wife into something that they might, with another kind of luck, have had easy and early. I wanted to give them a kind of break that would put them on something like an even keel with the people they had always thought of as their bene-factors and friends. To do that, I invented these Italian scenes, and I invented them pretty much out of memory; for instance, the business of getting up very early to watch the market carts coming down the *Lugarno.* I didn't wake up. My wife, Mary, woke up, and then woke me up, and so we went out to look; that scene comes straight out of memory based on what we saw. So does the business of the visit to Borgo San Sepolcro and the looking at the Pierro paintings. So with the man on the road with the smashed hand. So, even, the standard tourist business of going and turning on the lights in the Carmine to look at the "Expulsion from the Garden" of Masaccio. These are all common tourist experiences. They were great to Larry and Sally Morgan because this was the first time they were out of the prison that polio had created for them. All of that Italian action wrote itself pretty fast. But none of it was designed to bring in crucifixion problems. Those just happened, and they happened, I think, happily enough. They seemed to fit, and since they did, I put them in. I didn't go after them. I found them. That's a long answer.

Interviewer: We've talked before about the confusion that arises when your readers fail to distinguish between author and narrator. Who knows? Maybe you could straighten those readers out once and for all.

Stegner: What does Wallace Stegner have to do with it? The very fact that some of my experience goes into the book is all but inescapable, and true for almost any writer I can name. Which is real and which invented is (a) nobody's business and (b) a rather silly preoccupation and (c) impossible to answer. By the time I'm through converting my life to fiction it's half fiction at least and maybe more. People come to me yet and say, "Oh, it's too bad about your son who drowned in that surfing accident." Because some of *All the Little Live Things* reflects my immediate circumstances, they assume all of it does. People ought to learn to read better than that. The kind of *roman à clef* reading which determines the biographical fact extracted from fiction is not a good way to read. Read the fiction. The life, like all kinds of other things, is just raw material for the fiction. Insofar as the life is usable, it's used; insofar as it's unusable, something else is used. When I get through a book that involves some aspects of my own experience, as this new one does, I often don't know myself what I invented and what I didn't.

Interviewer: Is that because you have made the experience real?

Stegner: It's because I have thought my way into it in fictional terms. Yes. But I never want the end product to be taken as autobiography or biography. Because it isn't. No. The moment

I would begin to say, "This fictional person is so-and-so," I would be lying in my teeth. My fictional people are no more real people than Larry Morgan is me. They are constructs with some relations and some roots in real life, but they are certainly not people. If I said they *were* people, real people would begin to say, "Well, you did me wrong," and they would have every reason to say so. But as long as my characters are constructs and understood to be such, I have only borrowed, shall we say, some characteristics and experience for fictional purposes —and I hope transformed them.

Interviewer: My own limited experience in creating fiction tells me I have no choice but to draw upon my own experience as well as that of my friends, parents, children, if I am going to shape character. Almost everything I write seems literally to be cowritten. When it comes right down to it, I sometimes feel as if I am stealing.

Stegner: Let me tell you something about stealing. You can't steal anything that isn't already yours—in a literary way. If you can surround it, understand it, comprehend it, it's yours, unless you steal word-for-word—which is another matter. If the material is yours and it fits your concepts and the growing pattern in a novel, then it's already yours.

Interviewer: Crossing to Safety is about the abiding friendship of two couples, and, to some degree, two American families. What holds and finally binds this western family and this eastern family together in your mind: their similarities or dissimilarities?

Stegner: Both. The thing that brings them together in the first place is the annealing force of a university faculty, the collegiality of a shared workplace and shared work. Any workplace is where you meet the people you're probably going to be with during a spell of your life. The two men are both trained for that particular job, they have been run through the same computer, organized for the study and teaching of literature. I even

make a little fun of that. It's a way of making your head work
in cliches, a way of filling you with echoes. I suppose Sid Lang
is fuller of echoes than Larry Morgan is, but when they find
that fantastic marble fun house in the mountains, it's Larry's
head that Coleridge invades. The two men are programmed
in the same way. Here we are talking about similarities.

They are different men in the sense that one of them is
western, one eastern, one is a producer and one a consumer.
One is a writer, and the other is a reader. Both are necessary
in the world. But the reader would like to be a writer, and
so there's a tinge of envy in his friendship. The writer would
like to be rich. There's a tinge of envy in his. Each has something the other would like and doesn't have. Those are
differences.

A friendship is a very elusive, slippery, multiple kind of
relationship. Though it may be instantaneous—what happens
in half an hour may last for life—it is very complex. Your question has to be answered with the word *both*. Both similarities
and differences tie them together. For one thing, the differences
in wealth, in resources, in luck, make the western couple for a
long time almost pensioners of their friends. They hate it, but
they would hate it worse if they were pensioners of people *not*
their friends.

The Langs do everything to cover up the fact that they are
being benefactors, being generous not only with their money
but with the way they disguise their generosity. Without the
generosity of the Langs, Larry and Sally Morgan simply couldn't
afford to have them as friends. The Langs' wealth is by no means
the kind of wealth that goes in for elaborate display, conspic-
uous consumption.

In fact, it's an austere, New Englandy, inherited wealth with
a lot of restrictions on it, wealth which chooses to give itself
away and disguise itself and do good with itself. That kind of
wealth does exist. I had to have the difference in resources
between those two families or the one family couldn't demonstrate its qualities as well as I wanted it to.

Interviewer: What is the basis for friendship? Do we only respond to those people who take an interest in us? That's a question your narrator, Larry, raises at least once. What's Wallace Stegner's personal view?

Stegner: I was writing that book to try to find out. I'm not sure I satisfied myself. It is very clear to me that I will forgive in a friend things I would denounce in someone not a friend. So clearly it's not actions, it's not what your friends do. It's what your friends are. And that is why friendship is as mysterious to me as love. You don't know what causes it, but it often happens very swiftly. It's some kind of discovery of commonality, of mutual, shared emotions, feelings, not necessarily experiences. People's experiences are very different. But their feelings are alike. Friends must have something like the same value system. It's hard to know how that reveals itself, unless it reveals itself in actions. So here we are back again. Maybe it *is* what they do. I'm not sure I can answer your question at all except to say that I think real friendship is relatively rare in most people's lives. You may have hundreds of acquaintances and people that you speak of as "friends," but the ones you want when the chips are down may be very few in number: three or four. And they are likely to last for life. They are the people you want to keep track of; if you don't keep track of them, and they of you, there's something wrong with the friendship. Something has happened to it.

What causes friendship? I know more about what breaks it up. One of the things that breaks it up is the fact that the friend you had when you were fifteen, let us say, goes on running a service station and you take a Ph.D. and go on to teach at Harvard. It's very hard. The difficulty may be more from the friend who hasn't moved than from the one who has. The one who has moved on may be perfectly willing to come back to resume what made them friends at the age of fifteen, but the one who didn't is always going to be uneasy because he stayed in that place and didn't grow, and he feels the difference. That's an unhappy situation.

Interviewer: Yeah. Bruce Mason *in* Recapitulation, *for example, never actually looks up his old friend, Joe Mulder. He debates with himself, but your ambassador finally decides against knocking on that suburban Salt Lake City door.*

Stegner: Since I do everything by trial and error, I confess that I wrote scenes in which Bruce rang that doorbell and went on inside and met Joe and Joe's wife.

Interviewer: Pretty awkward, huh?

Stegner: Yes. I even experimented with having Joe married to Bruce's old girl. Several people have said, "Oh, why didn't you write that?" Well, I did. It didn't work. Finally, it just seemed to me that Bruce would be afraid. I meant him to be inhibited and maimed in certain ways. He never fully recovered from those traumas of his youth. As a matter of fact, I had done pretty much the same thing in *Angle of Repose* when Susan heads east from Boise to see her friend, Augusta, and finally, from Chicago or somewhere, Susan writes and says, "I can't. It wouldn't be me." I must think that happens to people; that's twice I've had friends turn away from a reunion after a long period of separation.

Interviewer: Does it bother you to think you might be repeating yourself?

Stegner: I didn't realize I had repeated myself until this minute. You tend to fear repetition when you get to a certain age because you've heard so many people tell the same stories, sometimes five times in an evening, and you don't want to get that way. In this case, I wasn't aware of repeating myself, yet I clearly did.

Interviewer: How important are literary friendships? How important are friends to a writer?

Stegner: I would hate to think that friends were simply purpose-servers, utilitarian. There's no question at all that literary conversation with people who know what they're talking about and whose books you have read, with whom you have some kind of friendly occupational relationship, is important. When you read a book, you're bound to get a glimpse of people that's closer than a lot of the glimpses you get in real life. And so literary conversation, the companionship of people of like minds, is very pleasurable. I wouldn't want to think of it strictly as a useful business, although once in a while it happens that way. Malcolm Cowley has helped me a time or two with his wisdom.

Interviewer: Do you consider him a friend?

Stegner: Oh, yes. One of the best. I was writing *Wolf Willow*, and I couldn't make it come together. It was an anthology in the first place. And Malcolm said, "Let me look at it," which was very friendly of him, and he looked and he said, "You know, I think if you just move this Dump Ground chapter from the beginning to the end"—or vice versa, I've forgotten which —"the book will come together better." And it did, like a puzzle when you find the key piece. I had a blind spot he did not have. So there is often a great usefulness in literary friends, but that isn't what you have them for. You don't have any friend *for* anything. You just have him. Or her.

Interviewer: What others do you think of as literary friends?

Stegner: I don't have many because I haven't lived a literary life. Most writers either live in New York or their own pieces of the hinterlands. Frank O'Connor was a good and close friend. So is Storm Jameson. But most of my literary friends are friendly acquaintances or ex-students—a separate category.

Interviewer: Do the women in your fiction seem to you stronger than the men? Doesn't your fiction address this question frequently? Are

*women stronger than men as a rule? By "stronger" I mean physio-
logically as well as psychologically. I'm thinking, too, of one of your
critics who claims your novels use women but are ultimately about men.*

Stegner: I wouldn't think such a generalization would be easy.
There are some women in my fiction, like the discombobulated
woman in *A Shooting Star*, who are not strong characters. I've
known a lot of women particularly in the more distant past,
not within the last twenty-five years, but back a ways: attractive,
well-educated, with nothing to do. Simply brought up and
well-educated to a dead end. Society wives. That kind often
end up alcoholics or something else self-destructive. They can't
be called strong characters.

I think Elsa in *Big Rock Candy Mountain*, who has a good
many qualities in common with my mother, is a strong character, stronger than her husband, who is a lot more active and
in some ways more imaginative. In *Angle of Repose* I would
guess that it's about a standoff. Susan is more talented in many
ways than Oliver. She shows off better. But as I wrote that
book, thinking that I was writing about her as a heroine, I came
to the end of it thinking maybe he is the hero because there is a
flaw in her, a flaw of snobbery. She doesn't adequately appreciate
the kind of person he is, or the kind of work he does. That's a
story not about either men or women but about a relationship,
a novel about a marriage.

This latest novel is, likewise, about a complicated relationship,
a relationship between two couples. The strongest person in it
is apparently Charity Lang. Also the most misguided, the one
who is ultimately her own defeat. But I don't know what
strength consists of. Actually it takes a good deal of strength
to be a Sid. He looks like a weakling and gets walked on, and
bossed, but he's very, very stable in a way, as strong as she is.
I don't know. I hope I don't make the kind of distinctions
between the sexes that would lead me into error.

I have been lucky, in some ways. My mother was a very
strong woman, and I got an example of the kind of patience

and endurance that even an unlucky woman can display. And I was lucky in writing *Angle of Repose* because the record was so complete. I couldn't have been a Victorian gentlewoman without taking a lot of material out of the letters of Mary Hallock Foote, who was, in her way, a quite remarkable character. So. Women sometimes ask me, "How do you know so much about women?" I don't know anything about women. I'm writing about people. It's not as if only women can write about women or men about men. After all, neither *Madam Bovary* nor *Anna Karenina* was written by a woman. I know novels about men written by women that are perfectly strong and true. I don't want to dismiss the sexes or dismantle them. I just don't want to choose between them.

Interviewer: In your new novel the two couples head off into the Vermont wilds anticipating a few days in paradise. Your character, Charity Lang, goes off with Pritchard's Field Guide *in one hand and a compass in the other, insisting that the trip be conducted "by the book." Charity seems to profit little from the experience even after she forces the company into a literal quagmire. Are you intentionally throwing kerosene on those feminist fires some of your critics seem to be tending? Only men belong in the woods?*

Stegner: No, I'm only writing a book. I'm letting the chips fall where they happen to fall. Charity is obviously not all women. She's not even very many women. But she is a woman. This woman I conceived of as very orderly—extremely organized —she organizes everything, every minute of the day. So she would organize the camping trip—and her way of organizing the trip would be to go to what she thought was an authority and follow the authority. The authority happens to be some half-assed boy scout. And she follows the authority into all kinds of preposterous situations.

Interviewer: Yes, but the others let her.

Stegner: She's not the kind of person you can prevent. But she does, at the end of that scene, when she's decided that three minutes over a low fire is not going to cook the chicken, admit she's made a mistake. Once in a while she can do that, because she's not small. She's just organized—overorganized. And dominating. She's the kind of woman who would put her children at the table and say, "Eat that spinach, and don't leave the table until you've eaten it." The kid could sit there for five hours.

Interviewer: Yes, just as the son, Paul, does in Norman's novel, A River Runs Through It. In fact, reading your novel, I kept asking myself the same question I asked about Maclean's book, "Does this novel have an antagonist?"

Stegner: No. I don't think it does. Not unless the antagonist is Fate or Karma. Character is Fate. The trouble here is that Charity has qualities which produce, in different situations, both good and bad. Each of the four I suppose has such qualities, but Fate comes in on them. Sally contracts polio. I put the polio in partly to show how unselfishly generous Charity could be, which she was. I didn't want Charity just imposing her will on people and becoming a martinet. Her iron will had to have good consequences as well. She stands off the doctors, helps out the nurses. She takes Sally to Warm Springs and makes sure that treatment gets carried out. So I don't think there is a personalized antagonist. The snake that I saw in that Eden was obviously this quality in Charity.

Interviewer: But is Charity capable of love?

Stegner: I think so, but only from the saddle.

Interviewer: For instance, in one of the Wisconsin sections of the novel, someone wonders if Charity is capable of picking up one of her own children and hugging the child for simply being itself.

Stegner: I guess I had very clearly in mind a certain time spirit. There was a time in the thirties when all of the guidebooks for bringing up children said, "Don't baby them. Let them bawl. Don't pick them up and cuddle them." That was literally what the books taught, and Charity would have gone to the books. We had this same problem, because the books said not to fondle a child, not to pick it up when feeding it, and all that. Now the advice is the exact opposite, and it's better advice. In the thirties Gesell and the others were the authorities that Charity would have gone to, and she would have followed their advice with absolutely scrupulous care. Again there is a kind of New England/ Puritan rigidity and austerity that I thought matched both the place and the time. Capable of love? She might be yearning for this baby all the time, but she would think it her duty *not* to pick it up.

Interviewer: So there is a point where a writer's consciousness ought to take over his intuitive responses, when the character begins to cast a longer shadow on the page and assume symbolic values? I'm thinking of the evolutionary process: first by accident, then by design.

Stegner: Oh, I suppose. Again, I would insist that those patterns are discovered and not imposed. When a writer finds them he helps them along. You would be foolish not to play any scene that is given you to play. Benny DeVoto said, in effect, "You run out your hits as far as you can. You don't stop on second." But the author's consciousness—certainly it ought never to be obvious. It's imposed, of course it's imposed. But the author's view of his own characters may be arrived at through a long period of inductive thinking about them. You don't put placards up for the reader saying, "This is my meaning."

The whole business of writing is an attempt to arrive at truth insofar as you can see it, so far as your capacity to unearth it permits. Truth is to be handled gingerly. That's an egg with a very thin shell. I'm not writing fables—where the moral is literally part of the form—I'm writing something from which the

reader is supposed to deduce or induce any moral that's there.
The moral value ought to be hiding in the material. I think you
have to be careful not to manipulate the material so that the
reader will go confidently to the piano and lift up the lid and
find the moral you've hidden there for him to find. Any book
that's worth anything ought to be read and thought over. And
when you think it over there ought to be something in it by
way of truth. I would hardly go any further than that.

*Interviewer: Does what you're saying, then, about the author's con-
sciousness hold true for the novel's particulars? Can we go back to a
question I raised the last time we picked up this interview? I pointed
out to you a few the possibilities for the first name of your narrator,
Lyman, in* Angle of Repose, *one of the possibilities being that of
a "whitewasher" or "Lie-Man." You denied making any conscious
association in your own mind. I went back to Tucson, laid out the
possibilities to a woman I met at a conference, who then unconsciously
or consciously included them in her article on your book.*

Stegner: I never thought of that pun on Lyman's name until you
suggested it to me, so if it was unconscious on my part, it was
totally unconscious. I think you've been misled in your youth.
Such things seem to me a form of gamesmanship and pedantry
I really don't want to play.

Lang, for instance, in the new novel is just a name. I don't
know where that came from. I wanted a Scottish name. It came,
I suppose, because I happened to run across Andrew Lang, a
translator of certain Greek classics. "Lang" is just a Scotch name.
It might as well have been McDermit.

*Interviewer: But it wasn't McDermit! It was Lang. What about the
name Ward, the family name in* Angle of Repose? *It seems patently
obvious to me that Lyman and his whole family are literal as well as
symbolic orphans. Lyman considers himself both a cultural guardian
and watchman, as well as a dependent. He, at least, is aware of
himself as a dependent or ward.*

Stegner: Well, I suppose I'm entitled to anything you can find in me. I'll accept that. But I'm certainly not doing anything like that on purpose. If I were Vladimir Nabokov, that's the kind of game I might play. I'm a very different kind of writer.

Interviewer: Very well, then, have it your way. The writer is unconscious and it's the reader who strays. Come awake and wave your magic and prophetic wand over this conversation for a moment. How well will the new novel be received? We're talking in January of 1987. Random House plans to release the novel in September, a date that will mark your fiftieth year as a published novelist. Where will the reviews appear, and what will your critics say?

Stegner: I haven't any idea that this novel is keyed to the preoccupations of the 1980s. I'd be very happy if it did make some noise, but I have no way of predicting whether or not it will. Once or twice, when I have had the notion that I had one to stick up there where they would notice it, they haven't noticed, so there's nothing I can do but wait and see. If they do me ill, then I'll grumble and sulk. And if they do me good, I will smile and be happy.

Interviewer: Oh, come off your lily pad! This is one of your finest novels. And it must be outright unnerving to write a book like, say, Angle of Repose *and then watch the* New York Times *ignore it, even when the Pulitzer committee nods benevolently. So what did you do then? A simple "sulk" and "brood"?*

Stegner: Yeah. I was made aware of the situation by all kinds of friends of mine, including many in the East, who kept writing to the *Times* and saying, "When are you going to review this book, because it's a book we admire very much?" Eventually, months later, the *Times* ran a retrospective review, which was a little condescending and kind of snobby. I don't know. The reasons they ignored it could have been personal. It might have had something to do with all kinds of things. Wright Morris and I talk about which one of us is the more neglected. We compete for the role. Neither of us wants it.

Interviewer: Well, that's just ducky. But then, after Angle of Repose, *you published* The Spectator Bird *and won a National Book Award. Did the* Times *review it? Do you want to know the answer?*

Stegner: No. They didn't.

Interviewer: Believe me, I'm not trying to make a hate object out of the Times. *Without it I'd be dead, living where and as I do.*

Stegner: Yes. That's all history, water under the bridge. Let's not bring anything on with a rain dance. *The Los Angeles Times* didn't review *The Spectator Bird* either. That, I found out later, was because Robert Kirsch, the book editor, was abroad and terminally ill, and somebody in his place just overlooked something. I wouldn't make a case for the *L.A. Times* being unfriendly, because they *have* been friendly. They've given me a prize. These things seldom happen through calculated neglect.

Interviewer: O.K., so much for the sky being uncloudy all day. The last time we spoke formally for the record, you mentioned the disadvantages of age to a writer. Very well. But are there no advantages whatsoever?

Stegner: Oh, of course there are. There are even advantages to being fifty years in the business of writing books, because one hand has a tendency to wash the other. People know one book and get reminded of another. A reputation is, to some extent, an accumulative affair. I suppose that's the best kind of reputation, one you've earned over a long period of time. That's the kind I would covet, if I were coveting.

Interviewer: I just wanted to make sure you were being balanced in your judgment about the question of writing fiction into an advanced age. The last time we spoke you groaned about the amount of time it took you to write fiction, that you were writing less quickly than you once did. "Yes," I thought, "but if he only keeps on a page a day, if he only salvages one page a day for a year . . ."

Stegner: Yes, one page would be pretty good. There are advantages. You should know more. You should be able to estimate people better. You should have, if not a more mellow, at least a less distorted view of the world. But a lot of the business of writing books is, as Hemingway said, selling energy. The disadvantage of age is that your energy level goes down. You have less to sell. And eventually the level goes down so far you haven't any to sell, and you quit writing books.

Interviewer: Oh, sure. That's what you said last time! Off the record you said, "I don't know if I'm going to have another novel."

Stegner: Well, all right. I'll go on like a fool until I'm ninety —and then wish I hadn't. Wishing I hadn't written the last three. There are other things that happen when you get to be my age. Literary fashions change, leaving you stranded.

Interviewer: Fine. I'll just leave you stranded with poor old Sophocles who lived to be ninety and wrote Oedipus at Polonus—

Stegner: Still, at my age you care less. You just plain care less. You get tired of people's problems, and you take less interest in them. You think, "Oh, to hell with them. I'll go out and tend to the garden." The kinds of problems you can care about in your old age are different from the kinds of problems you care about when you're thirty. And they are probably different from the kinds of problems most of your readers care about. So you tend to move away from all the heat and calamity of living and get into a kind of serenity that is not very creative.

Interviewer: That's one option. But let me tell you something about

*America and American readers. We now have more people over the
age of sixty-five in the United States than ever before. On the average,
thirty people a day hit the century mark in terms of personal age. As a
nation we are at once growing younger and older. I don't give a damn
what the marketing people say. I know which group not only reads but
buys the most fiction—serious fiction, I mean. But answer my next
question. If you could literally go back and change anything, would
you do it?*

Stegner: Oh, I don't know. It's a kind of fruitless speculation,
isn't it?

*Interviewer: Maybe. Not necessarily for a novelist, I would think.
Besides, I'm the one who's supposed to be asking the questions.*

Stegner: If I could go back? There are many, many things I
would do differently if I could go back. Of course. I would go
back and study different things. If we're in the self-improvement
business, which we seem to be on the basis of this last book,
there are many ways I could improve myself.

Interviewer: You would study biology and anthropology.

Stegner: Yeah. I would study both of those. I would waste far
less time than I wasted when I—

*Interviewer: Oh, bushwah! You've produced fifty or more books in
as many years. Where did you waste a second of time and when? You
skipped two grades in school, landed at the university at age sixteen.
You went from Wisconsin to Harvard once you began teaching. And
from Harvard to Stanford. How is that wasting time?*

Stegner: By that time I wasn't wasting it. I'm thinking up to the
time I was about twenty—twenty-two, maybe—no, twenty.
You waste your youth. I wasted mine working too much. I
fiddled.

Interviewer: Be more specific.

Stegner: I played a lot of cards, for one thing.

Interviewer: Cards? Like pinochle, bridge? What?

Stegner: Like solo. I spent a lot of time reaching
for spread misères.

Interviewer: What?

Stegner: You know. It's a lay-down hand in solo. " 'I guess
I'll make it a spread misère,' said Dangerous Dan McGrew."
I suppose I didn't waste a lot of time, but I was a frivolous
youth. I really was.

Interviewer: But isn't that what youth is for?

Stegner: It doesn't seem so. I had plenty of reasons to be
serious. If I could go back, I would waste less. And I would
waste less of it at frivolous and unproductive work. I worked
my way through college being a clerk in a rug-and-linoleum
store forty hours a week. There was nothing in that work that
taught me anything. I did it for a long time—and was glad to
do it, because it was the only way to go to school. If I were
going back, I'd find some other way. There were so many
books I wanted to know and would know now if I hadn't
worked those forty-hour weeks out of my life.

*Interviewer: How much of yourself do you find in Charity Lang? She
certainly wastes no time in your new novel, least of all when she's dying.*

Stegner: Very little. I'm not that systematic, and I find it a little
difficult to be indefinitely dominating. I catch up with myself
now and again. Her problem is that most of the time she doesn't.

But I would like to be as generous and as thoughtful of others as Charity is.

Interviewer: Do you recall these words? "Nobody has quite made a western Yoknapatawpha County or discovered a historical continuity comparable to that which Faulkner traced from Ikkemotubbe the Chickasaw to Montgomery Ward Snopes. Maybe it isn't possible, but I wish someone would try. I might even try myself." Fess up. Have you been trying?

Stegner: Not systematically, no. When I wrote that statement, sometime in the fifties maybe, I was wishing that somebody could do it, and I suppose I was becoming aware that in many people's eyes, and perhaps in my own, I was becoming a western writer, and I was curious to know what that meant, curious to know if it was some kind of fence I was stuck inside of. If I was going to be stuck inside the fence, what was I going to do with the territory inside the fence? I pretty well decided, then or later, that the territory was a little too vast and various, that you couldn't make a Yoknapatawpha County out of it. There was not enough homogeneity in the material.

I don't know how systematic Faulkner was in writing the Yoknapatawpha County. I suspect he wasn't a systematic kind of man, but he was dealing with material that was homogeneous, that related one book to another, and characters from one book to another, and through three generations of a family of characters. In the West, there isn't any such continuity, none of those kinds of continuities to deal with, even if I wanted to. And if I had been tempted to try to make some kind of saga like that, I couldn't possibly have done it without confining myself to a particular part of the West, Salt Lake City, say, or Saskatchewan, Montana, parts of the West I knew. Here we run again into the lack of a usable past. There wasn't enough in those places to produce that kind of saga—I thought. So, I'm scattered. Even when I'm writing about the things I know,

the books that I related to western matters, I'm inevitably
scattered. The only things I was able to do in the way of relat-
ing were to write a trailer to *The Big Rock Candy Mountain* in
Recapitulation, to write two Joe Allston books and another little
Joe Allston novella about this part of contemporary California.
That's not a saga. That's only a minimal crystallization and
coagulation. All of Faulkner's people tend to revolve around
the courthouse square, the Confederate monument. It's a different, much more concentrated country in the South. It's a
rural tradition with a relatively homogeneous population,
homogeneous problems—the problem of slavery and its
consequences—it's a rural society and notably traditional.

*Interviewer: One of your critics writes, Stegner "reminds me of Faulkner,
a mythologizer notoriously unreliable in his comments about his own
work . . . Stegner treats myth and tradition as does Faulkner, who
uses them 'in terms which absolutely surround them and encompass
them and melt them down and make them into something else . . .
(who) transcends and transforms his tradition.'"*

Stegner: Well, it would be nice to think I have all those powers.
I don't understand, really, what she's talking about. I am, so far
as I know, unaware of myth in my work—notoriously unreliable as I am. Again, I have to say that if she finds these things in
my fiction, I'm happy, but I don't quite know what she's talking
about. I have been, as you suggest, trying to make a historical
continuity between past and present, but I don't understand
that as myth. I understand that only in terms of trying to match
past and present, simply as continuity, and I don't believe the
myth matches either past or present. The mythic western is
pure hokum. It applies to very small numbers of people over
very short periods of time and not at all to nine-tenths of the
people who lived here. It is personification of Individualism
and Self-Reliance that produce those myths. I guess I like
things that are closer to the actual facts of experience.

In a way, I'm opposed to myth, if you come right down to

it. I don't like the company there. I'm not trying to make Hercules or Shane in my fiction. I'm just trying to make Bo Mason, people like that.

Interviewer: Have you been conscious of attempting to debunk the myths, especially the American gospels you just mentioned or statements like "Rain follows the plow . . . Gold is anywhere you stick your shovel"?

Stegner: I'd call those delusions, not myths. But, sure. I grew up doubting the big-bonanza–just-over-the-next-rise notion, because for years I watched my family chase it. I got pretty jaundiced on that subject. A little realism would have helped my family a good deal. Instead of expecting to make a big strike somewhere, which is a very good American notion, encouraged by free land, by opportunity, by freedom of action or nearly complete freedom of action, I would have liked to see a little more just plain stick-to-it-iveness at times. The longest journey begins with a single step—I believe that more than I believe in the fortune over the next rise. I could see my father always refusing to make the first step. He always wanted the step to be a hundred-yard broad jump. Broad jumping is not the way you travel. It leads to a succession of falls.

Interviewer: Maybe it takes more than one generation to make a man. Your father left you behind. That's rather positive, isn't it?

Stegner: Sure. My father left many people behind because he was running backwards.

Interviewer: Is it possible for a writer to open up "new" territory for fiction?

Stegner: Mmmmmmmmmm. It may be possible to open up new territory for fiction, but not new ways of getting at—. Insofar as fiction is the record of human action, human actions are not necessarily changed by technology. *Star Wars* and *Star Trek* don't change the human action. They only change the machinery. "No new ways to be new," as Frost said. I think that's a reasonably good statement. "There's nothing new under the sun," sayeth the Preacher. "All the rivers run into the seas, but the seas are not full." I think more circularly than linearly. I don't think there are beginnings and destinations so much as circles which end by closing the circle and starting over again. I can't think of any fiction that introduces new elements of what used to be called "Human Nature," nothing that isn't present, say, in *The Iliad* and *The Odyssey*, if we're speaking of novels. The qualities of character, the machinery of suspense and climax, of mounting action and falling action: I don't think we've seen anything new in that way. There are new clothes, because civilization can change, and we get out of armor and into doublet and hose and then Brooks Brothers pants, but we're still the same people and doing the same things, essentially. I think it's a mistake to think originality amounts to that much.

I know people, for instance, including former students of mine, who got into the sexual revolution and thought they had opened up really new material for fiction. They felt like Renaissance men and women discovering a New World with fifty-seven positions. But it's there in *1001 Nights*, it's there in the *Satyricon* of Petronius, it's there—though not so commonly or so publicly—in a whole library of books. There's nothing new about it. I doubt there's much of it that Cain didn't know as soon as he got acquainted East of Eden. I don't think that's a way of getting anywhere: to pretend that there's anything new to be said. What's important is a larger understanding of what has always been. I believe some things have been added in that respect.

Interviewer: Like what?

Stegner: I suppose depth psychology may have give us both new soil and new tools. Though I'm not sure I've ever seen an Id —and I would go running in another direction if I ever did. Freud's theory of the personality doesn't always strike me as plausible. I'm half-inclined to agree with Nabokov on the subject of Freud: a great witch doctor. And I would have to say that I doubt psychoanalysis therapy has produced many cures, though it has produced a good many novels.

I don't mean to say the species is absolutely incapable of change. What I mean to say is that what we change to may have already been there but neglected. Aldo Leopold's American Land Ethic is, in some ways, for example, prefigured in Stoic philosophy. Marcus Aurelius: "What's bad for the beehive can't be good for the bee." It's certainly there in a lot of St. Francis, there in Zen, in American Indian religions: that attitude toward the earth that is respectful and reverent, that goes with the flow of the earth instead of contrary to it. So I don't think that if we all adopted Leopold's land ethic tomorrow we would be doing anything new. We might be going in a different direction from the one we're headed toward, but it wouldn't be a new direction, only a change of direction, one already inscribed in the books.

It may sound hopeless, the way I put it, but I don't feel hopeless. I just don't expect ever to be an innovator. Innovation doesn't happen in those areas. Innovation happens in technology. Innovation happens in industry. It doesn't happen in human affairs, or, really, in art.

Interviewer: Is it possible for a writer to protect the places he or she loves by writing about them?

Stegner: It doesn't help to write about them in celebratory ways because all you do is stimulate the tourist industry.

I have sometimes carefully avoided writing in a celebratory way about places I love on the earth. On the other hand, you can write, as Leopold did, about attitudes and responses to the earth and do some educating. The problem is not wickedness, evil. Lynn White calls it a development of the Judeo-Christian tradition which makes man the center of the earth and makes all creatures subservient to him. The problem, as stated in Genesis, is a piece of early Jewish arrogance. But many people have felt it. The Navajo call themselves Diné, the People. Many, many people have called themselves *the* people, as if no other people existed, have thought of themselves as the center of the universe. I think we have to get over that. I am profoundly of the opinion *that* attitude has to go or we destroy our own habitat. So without innovating anything, I would just rather get a little more American Indian than Judeo-Christian in my attitudes toward the earth, and a little more Zen and St. Francislike in my attitude toward other animals.

Interviewer: You've observed that the "new man" Crèvecoeur defined had become something else by the time James got around to writing The American. *Having lived through the 1910s, '20s, '30s, '40s, '50s, '60s, '70s, and now the 1980s, is there anything you can tell us that might help the species survive?*

Stegner: I've been trying to do that in a lot of different ways and in a lot of different books. Crèvecoeur's notion is touched by the Rousseauvian idea of the naturally good human being given new opportunity. And new opportunity—Crèvecoeur never got around to saying this—is often abused. People take advantage of it to extend beyond their normal appetites. I think Wendell Berry is right when he said we've gone about as far as we *can* go with that American notion, the New Man in a new country. It's time to change direction and quit thinking of the American as simply an animated economic opportunity. That's Ronald Reagan's way of looking at America. I'm profoundly opposed to enterprise when enterprise is uncontrolled by any notion of the public good. In the case of the Ronald Reagans of the world, there is no notion of the public good, of the *polis*, the way in which people relate one to another. Instead, we find Individualism gone berserk. I don't know if you're

familiar with a book called *Habits of the Heart*, the title of
which comes from Tocqueville. It's an examination of American attitudes, of individualism without what Wendell Berry
calls "membership," without association, without a notion of a
polis, which results, according to Robert Bellah, in a lifestyle
that changes as often as the coat or tie, the absolute repudiation
of commitment or obligation to anything. You're not obligated
by religion, you're not obligated by a social conscience, you're
not obligated by family: you change your family, you get a
divorce and start over. You're not even obligated to stay with
one sex. You're absolutely free. And absolutely, it seems to me,
in a vacuum. I would agree with Bella that that kind of individualism gone berserk, gone rampant, leads down some cold
ninth circle of hell. You know that's no way that any people
can continue to live. We had better get over precisely the kind
of thing Ronald Reagan urges us to get back to.

How did this get political?

*Interviewer: Who knows? Let's switch subjects. I understand your
reticence to take credit for the accomplishments of those writers who came
through Stanford as students. But you also wave a hand of dismissal to
the whole idea that T. H. Watkins raises in a recent article: that you've
been one of "the central figures in the modern conservation movement."
You worked for Udall in the Kennedy administration; before that as an
active freelancer in DeVoto's camp; and you've been on the advisory
boards for National Parks, Historical Sites, Buildings and Monuments,
as well as on the Governing Council of the Wilderness Society. Pity
the outsiders reading this interview and quit boxing your ankles before
I aim a kick at your shins. You were waging war to protect the environment before most of us were in short pants. How much of an insider
have you been?*

Stegner: Not really an insider at all. I told Tom Watkins, and
I would repeat: I am not a good soldier in the environmental
armies because I don't seem to work well in bodies with other
people. Here's an irony. I'm against individualism gone rampant,

but I don't actually seem to be a very good team player. I feel that the team strategies are constantly running across what I am doing at the moment and feel I ought to be and must be doing. I guess I must admit sometimes I rear back in the breaching a little when others are urging me along. I become recalcitrant. Even when I agree wholeheartedly with the people who are urging me along, I don't like to be pushed. So some of the work of conservation, which is by necessity touched with zealotry, I resist. I'm not fooling when I tell Tom I'm not really a good team player. I have the complete conviction and conversion, but I seem to have to do it on my own. That means I write when I feel it and not when the tactics of the moment call for it.

I have been unable to bring much of my thought about conservation into fiction, because I suspect myself when I begin to be doctrinaire. I guess I must hold the integrity of the material to be of greater value than any message that I might at the time want to get across. If the material itself dictates that message, it would be in there, but I don't seem to be able to put it in by force or will, because that seems to me a dilution of the essential.

Interviewer: But it does surface in your fiction, don't you see? Plenty of public servants turn up: John Wesley Powell, for instance, although in that case you were doing nonfiction, as in the case of your DeVoto biography. But Bruce Mason is a public servant. Oliver Ward has a kind of civic-mindedness he shares with Powell.

Stegner: And something in common with Bo Mason, too, the spoiled frontiersman. Oliver's notion of how to be a public servant in the West was a mistaken notion, but he did have the notion of public service. His notion was building a dam that he hoped would do a lot of good. Well, I happen to be an antidam man, so I have to be against my own character in a way. Oliver is not a Bo Mason, but neither is he a Powell. Even Powell I would have to disagree with on certain things because he didn't live long enough to see what the development of the dry country would do to it. If he had lived long enough, he probably would have made mistakes. We all would and do. He had in his time a better grasp than anybody around.

Interviewer: What about your friend Ansel Adams? Did you side with him on the question of nuclear energy?

Stegner: It's possible that there is no form of energy, nuclear energy included, which will be without environmental consequences. Ansel thought that nuclear energy was likely to be without pollution consequences of the kinds that spoil air and water. I'm afraid there are other consequences even worse. Do we back up—something the human race has never done—from a high technology to a lower technology, or do we accept the consequences? As far as I'm concerned, the only thing we can do is to do the best we can do in every given circumstance and try to minimize the consequences, think about the consequences before we undertake the new technology. Dams are not the way in the West any more. For one thing, they're too temporary. Power will have to come, increasingly, from other sources. Irrigated agriculture, too, is very definitely an agriculture with time limits on it. Insofar as the West is an agricultural economy, it is definitely a doomed one, unviable over an extended period of time. The dams will silt up and the fields will go saline. Agriculture will have to move back to Iowa or somewhere it belongs. And the Central Valley will have to go back to sunflowers—sooner or later—or to the deserts we will make there. But that's thinking in very long-range terms, and I am perfectly aware of the human disruption and hardship that would be brought about if irrigation agriculture were suddenly brought to a halt. My God, that would depopulate the West, or three-quarters of it, but it would also have very serious consequences for large parts of the earth, so I think getting out of what we have gotten ourselves into is a very serious and complicated problem. Atomic power is one example. There is a limited fuel supply for any kind of power; there are kinds of pollution and damage that any kind of energy production brings; if we go on producing power in the old ways until the dams silt up, the fuel runs out, or the poisons get too thick, we definitely accept a shorter term future for the whole country and the whole society and the whole civilization.

I don't know where I'd stand in relationship to Ansel on the question of atomic power. I don't like nuclear power, but I don't like some other forms of power generation, either. The Harvard Group determined that conservation of power and the maximum use of solar energy is the best way to go for the time being. As far as I know, there are no consequences of solar, tidal, or wind energy. I believe you can think small and get a lot of your energy from wind. Advocates for thinking small have brought about in New England, say, good consequences. A lot of old dams that used to power grist mills and were later abandoned have opened up again. They turn one or two little turbines. That power is going into local places without ruining the environment. Those streams are not, by and large, eroding streams, because that's a relatively clean country with grass and turf and woods.

In the West dams pose far more problems. And we haven't gone in for little dams, either. I guess by and large I'm half an enemy of the civilization I belong to, and that's an awkward way to be. I don't believe in unlimited manipulation of the earth or the earth's forces. I'd rather manipulate less and have fewer gadgets.

Interviewer: Can you give us a reading list of neglected books of this or any other century that ought to be required reading?

Stegner: An impossible question to answer. For one thing, I wouldn't know how neglected they were. For another thing, I'm not the man to make such a list in the first place.

Interviewer: How much anthropology have you read?

Stegner: Not an awful lot. Probably a lot of anthropology that

is bad anthropology. Some ethnology. Ardrey and people like
that. Lorenz. A lot of individual digging in the Southwest.
Emil Haury. But I'm not very well read in anthropology and
archeology. Levi-Strauss I find hard going. A very good friend
of mine was for years director of the Pennsylvania Museum of
Archeology. They dug all kinds of things all over the world,
Sybaris and Gordias's Tomb and Tikal. I've been familiar
with many digs from knowing my friend.

Interviewer: What about physics?

Stegner: Physics I don't try to read. I have a lot of friends in
the Stanford Physics Department, and some of them Nobel
winners. If you can learn from anybody, you ought to be able
to learn from them. But my head isn't meant for it. Biology
I have tried, not always with understanding. The kinds of
physicists I know are all either particle physicists of the most
advanced kind or else they are engineers who build the
machines the others do Nobel Prize experiments in. I
understand little of what they're doing. But I find them to
be very large-minded and humane men and women. I think
the understanding of their specialty is less important than my
understanding of them as persons. I'm a scientific illiterate.
I try to understand, but it's hopeless. I would hate, on the
other hand, to go through life without learning to
understand something about the double helix.

*Interviewer: What about Bergson? Did he influence
your own ideas about Time?*

Stegner: Maybe.

Interviewer: What about sociology?

Stegner: Some. Now and again sociologists forget history, I'm
afraid. They tend to look upon the scene before them. I made

some highly exaggerated remarks about sociology through Lyman Ward in the beginning of *Angle of Repose*. Lyman's son is a sociologist and tends to look upon the scene before his eyes as if it had been born full-blown and had no historical roots. If sociologists have a sense of history, it's obviously a very rewarding study. If they don't, then I think they're playing with mirrors.

Interviewer: Speaking of playing with mirrors, is the proliferation of creative writing programs on the nation's campuses in any way dangerous?

Stegner: Yes. It's dangerous because, if you'll pardon the expression, a lot of people in English departments should never be trusted to run a program. Their training is all in the other direction, all analytical, all critical. It's all a reader's training, not a writer's training, so they have no notion of how to approach the opportunity.

Interviewer: During the years you taught at Stanford, part of the time you shared the corridors with Ivor Winters, a formidable critic. Former students like Ed Loomis said they were "very much aware of dominions and borders that were taken very seriously in these little intellectual baronies. There was a certain amount of distrust—or perhaps dislike would be a more accurate characterization." How much distrust? How much dislike? To what advantages or disadvantages of the students?

Stegner: Ivor Winters was, as you say, a formidable critic, positive and often unyielding in his opinions, and intolerant of ideas that conflicted with his. He was not a man you could debate with, because he never debated, he asserted. On the other hand, he was learned, utterly serious, and a devoted teacher to those with whom he could work and who could work with him. We had our differences, which were never mortal, and we generally operated, as Ed Loomis suggests, by a division of territory. Ivor kept his poets close, away from contamination, with the result, which I never liked, that poets and fiction writers had too little contact. That situation has not applied since Ivor's retirement and death, and so far as I am able to observe, poets and fiction writers mix and blend and influence one another in the present-day program.

Interviewer: As a nation, are we pursuing the best course by subsidizing fiction writers and poets and the publication of their work through the auspices of the National Endowment?

Stegner: I suppose it could be said that arts that require public support don't justify themselves and should be allowed to wither. But the arts have always needed support, because they are a product of a highly evolved society with plenty of leisure, and few of them can count on a mass audience big enough to keep them solvent and flourishing. I have no difficulty with the spectacle of the federal government playing modest Maecenas. After all, when I was breaking in, there was outright support for the arts through the WPA, essentially a welfare program. The only problem is that a leaky tap will always attract lapping tongues. Any fellowship program, even such university programs as Stanford's, must keep a careful eye out for plausible fellowship lushes. Fellowships are best applied to young writers with big ambitions, to help them over the first hump. I don't know the hazards of other arts—I suspect composers have it worst —but any beginning artist needs time to develop, and fellowships, federal or otherwise, buy him time.

Interviewer: I understand Jackson Benson has been working toward a Wallace Stegner biography. I envy him the opportunity but pity him your natural reticence to make public what you insist on keeping private. You once dismissed my suggestion that you write an autobiography by saying, "Nothing ever happened to me but long hours upon my rump in front of a typewriter." How does it feel to know Benson is going to test that hypothesis? How cooperative are you being?

Stegner: The biography on which Benson is presently working is one of a series on "notable" westerners—a brief study concentrating on the career. Later, when I am out of his hair, he anticipates going on to a full-length biography. I don't have to be very actively cooperative in either project, but I expect to give him full access to my papers, such as they are.

Interviewer: What does Wallace Stegner do when he simply wants to relax—apart from reading and writing, teaching and lecturing, stumping for conservation?

Stegner: Walking, reading, gardening. I am past tennis because of a shoulder separation, past skiing because I hate the cold, and past being a beach bum for obvious reasons.

Interviewer: What role has Mary Stuart Page played in Wallace Stegner's life and career? Does she deserve any credit or blame?

Stegner: She has had no role in my life except to keep me sane, fed, housed, amused, and protected from unwanted telephone calls; also to restrain me fairly frequently from making a horse's ass of myself in public, to force me to attend to books and ideas from which she knows I will learn something; also to mend my wounds when I am misused by the world, to implant ideas in my head and stir the soil around them, to keep me from falling into a comfortable torpor, to agitate my sleeping hours with problems that I would not otherwise attend to; also to remind me constantly (not by precept but by example) how fortunate I have been to live for fifty-three years with a woman that bright, alert, charming, and supportive.

Interviewer: Another great American writer once wrote, "Death is the mother of beauty, mystical/Within whose burning bosom we devise/ Our early mothers waiting, sleeplessly." Is one life ever enough? How does one deal with the Grim Reaper moving toward him nearing eighty?

Stegner: I would like to think that one life is enough, and that when I see it coming to an end I can meet the darkness with resignation and perhaps acceptance. I have been lucky. I came from nowhere and had no reason to expect as much from this one life as I have got. I owe God a death, and the earth a pound or so of chemicals. Now let's see if I can remember that when the time comes.

Interviewer: In your only formal statement on your personal beliefs, you write, "I am terribly glad to be alive; and when I have wit enough to think about it, terribly proud to be a man and an American with all the rights and privileges that those words connote; and most of all I am humble before the responsibilities that are also mine. For no right comes without a responsibility, and being born luckier than most of the world's millions, I am also born more obligated." What new obligations and responsibilities do you feel confronting you now? Or are there any?

Stegner: No new ones—haven't we agreed with Frost that there are no new ways to be new?—but only reiterated and intensified versions of the old ones: the obligation to use oneself to the bone, to be as good as one's endowments and circumstances let one be, to project one's actions over and beyond the personal. The only things I owe to myself I owe to my notions of justice. But I owe a great deal, in the way not only of obligation but of tenderness, to my family and my friends. Chekhov said he worked all his life to get the slave out of himself. I guess I feel my obligation is to get the selfishness and greed, which often translates as the Americanism, out of myself. I want to be a citizen of the culture, of the best the culture stands for, not of a nation or a party or an economic system.

Interviewer: Where did Sid Lang disappear to during the final scene in your new novel?

Stegner: I don't know where he went. Does it matter? He went where he was sure of being alone. If he was hiding under a dead leaf or a stone it's all right with me.

Interviewer: What will be Wallace Stegner's next writing project?

Stegner: No new writing projects, beyond an introduction to the letters of Ansel Adams, whom I loved as a friend, respected as a moral force, and greatly admired as an artist.